THE WONDERFUL WEST

1. Our West was developed by generations of Americans who wanted to see what was on the other side of the mountain. Any mountain. Or, for that matter, any river. (*Grinnell Lake and Glacier, Montana*)

THE WONDERFUL WEST

STEWART H. HOLBROOK

DOUBLEDAY & COMPANY, INC.
Garden City, New York

Library of Congress Catalog Card Number 63–12346

Printed in the United States of America

CONTENTS

Books by Stewart H. Holbrook

The Wonderful West
Dreamers of the American Dream
Iron Brew: A Century of American Ore and Steel
The Yankee Exodus: An Account of Migration from New England
Ethan Allen: A Biography
The Story of American Railroads
Holy Old Mackinaw: A Natural History of the American Lumberjack
Lost Men of American History
Burning an Empire: America's Great Forest Fires
Little Annie Oakley and Other Rugged People
Far Corner: A Personal View of the Pacific Northwest
The Old Post Road
The Age of the Moguls
The Columbia

COLOR ILLUSTRATIONS

Color Illustrations

THE WONDERFUL WEST

INTRODUCTION

Chapter One

Many who live here will tell you that the American West came into being by reason of beaver or gold or an illusion commonly called the Northwest Passage. Any one of these notions will do to explain matters. And so, too, will an even greater simplification: Our West was due to the built-in curiosity of generations of Americans who merely wanted to see what was on the other side of the mountain. Any mountain. Or, for that matter, any river.

Just where the West begins depends a good deal upon where you are standing—where you drove your stakes. Though I drove mine more than forty years ago, not far from where the West begins to peter out in tidewater and the waves are coming in from China, I would not dream of telling anybody where the West begins. I have long since been housebroken in that regard.

Where the West begins is a delicate and far too important a subject to be settled by anything short of a national election. There are even degrees of West among Westerners. And although arguments concerning what is basically a matter of geographical status seldom reach the two-gun stage during recent years, the business of longitude west of Greenwich is stoutly supported by a vocabulary consisting chiefly of sneers: "And how is everything back here in the East?" asked the Walla Walla merchant, as he registered at the Hotel Cheyenne.

Yet, there are times when one is forced by circumstances to be specific about a region. This book happens to be such a one. And I choose to think that the Wonderful West I am writing about begins where the one-hundredth degree of longitude runs down through the Dakotas, Nebraska, Kansas, and Oklahoma. Let Texas care for its own wonderful state, and State of Mind. It just happens to be the only section I have never visited; and I fear I should thus fail to do it justice.

But, if only because British Columbia was the first landfall I made when I first came west of the Rockies, I should like to include this Canadian province in the Wonderful West. I can think of no place the adjective fits better on our side of the border.

When we come to the matter of describing the American West, I realize that the average Easterner, and perhaps the average European, would think it odd to map it from West to East, yet that is in keeping with the manner of its settlement. Oregon was a United States territory and California a state before any other political unit was formed. As for British Columbia, it became a Crown Colony in 1858, long before the Dominion of Canada came into existence and the prairie provinces—Alberta, Saskatchewan, and Manitoba—were still Prince Rupert's Land, a private trapping and trading preserve of the hoary old Hudson's Bay Company.

As of today, I'd rather not learn how many million people live in this Wonderful West. Let the hard-working realtors add them up, then repaint those city-population brags, posted near the highways, without which the least western hamlet has failed of its civic duty. Still, no matter where the masses of people have settled in large clumps, population west of the one-hundredth meridian is comparatively spotty. There remain vast sections of wilderness where no people live at all, and only the call of the owl and the cry of the coyote break the immense hush of solitude.

As a general thing, natives of the region are likely to think of it as "old," as long established; but the people who have come here from elsewhere tend to consider it romantically new country, still a part of America's Last Frontier.

After more than forty years of living and working here in the West, I feel a little self-conscious about the title of this book. During my time I have never thus referred to it, or any part of it, as "wonderful." After all, WHO said this is a wonderful country, out here where the West Begins and, for all practical purposes, Ends? For instance, what brought me here in 1920, and why is my home not only West of the Rockies but West of the Cascade Mountains? (Please note the implied and grossly invidious comparison of geographic features.) Before I go on about the West, this might be a good place to pause briefly, to see if I know why I came here; and why I remain.

When I crossed the Rockies for the first time, and came down the west slope to Vancouver, I was wearing the only derby hat in British Columbia. I had bought it in Boston on the day I purchased a railroad ticket that promised to take me to the West Coast and also return me, within a period of six months, to the Hub of the Universe. It was a thoroughly durable hat. Three years later I nailed it to a big fir stump in the British Columbia timber and took off for Oregon. By that time I had long since sold the return portion of my ticket to Boston.

I have never been quite certain what inspired me in the first place to come to the Northwest, unless it was to find out if those picture postcards of monstrous trees were fakes doctored up for the tourist trade. Nor am I sure I ever made up my mind to stay permanently in the West at all. I think the decision came so gradually that it could scarcely be considered one.

The analogy could be bettered, yet the effect of the West in my case reminds me of the antinicotine tracts read in my youth, which warned of the subtle and sinister spell cast by Tobacco. This, so it was made to appear, crept upon the innocent softly. Presently, however, he was enveloped, this Victim, with the captivating wreaths of smoke. And these, of course, turned out to be, in italics, the *Iron Bands of Vice*.

Well, I dutifully read the tracts, then joyfully welcomed the hideous habit much as later I read the booster pamphlets of various chambers of commerce which left the impression that one could have a decent living, here in the West, simply by eating the gorgeous scenery.

Despite these and other irritations, due mostly to overanxiety to impress the new arrival, I settled down to earn my keep as a reporter here where the buffalo roamed (in enclosures) and occasionally one even caught sight of deer and antelope at play.

If this is a pretty weak explanation of how the Wonderful West looked at least to one settler in God's Own Country, it will have to do. I can do no better, and was probably a pushover anyhow. I came here with no preconceived ideas. (Witness the derby hat.) Any notion of a Wild West operated by Indians, Cowboys, and Badmen derived from the Diamond Dick and Buffalo Bill literature of my teens, had long since been rubbed out. In recent years, however, I have known young men from the East—and even from states west of the Mississippi—to arrive in Oregon and California wearing gallon-size Stetsons and packing genuine Colt revolvers.

To the hogwash of Western movies has been added the hogwash of TV Westerns. These infamous libels on the American West generally concentrate on the Southwest. One may doubt that they alone have had much influence on migration westward, though the over-all Hollywood syndrome may well be attractive, even strongly magnetic, to the dedicated yearners who want to believe in an Old West that never existed.

This brings me to a long forgotten commentator on the West, the late Harry Campbell Freeman, formerly of Montana, who used to put it on the line in regard to the relationship between the two main divisions of the United States. These were the Wild & Woolly West and the Civilized & Effete East. Of Mr. Freeman I know little except he was a journalist familiar with the whole canon of the West and that in 1900 he wrote a book entitled *A Brief History of Butte, Montana, the World's Greatest Mining Camp.*

This book was a typical chamber-of-commerce job, acrawl with illustrations obviously paid for by every mining company in the area. Typical, that is, except for the Introduction, signed by Author Campbell at Butte, Montana, November 17, 1900. Here, sixty-two years ago, in the often flowery prose of the period, Western Booster Freeman displayed more common-sense knowledge of East vs. West than I've seen elsewhere since I moved from the one to make my home in the other.

Freeman liked to call it the Boundless West. Out of this region, he observed with full magisterial flavor, was coming, even as he wrote, a literature of every description concerning its resources, its development, life, grandeur of scenery, and "every phase that can possibly serve as a vehicle to relieve the mind."

One of these efforts, he went on, "emanates from the pen of the student of events, who sees the unfolding of mighty things which shall leave their imprint on the future of a great and growing nation." Next, it might be an article that "purports"—he chose the verb with care—that purports to be the work of the critic. This fellow, after a superficial study of prevailing conditions, Freeman charged, "finds much delight in exaggerating the primitiveness of Western institutions, the roughness of its life and the downright depravity of its public morality."

The trouble with this critic was that "he gave little or no thought to the obstacles which had to be overcome." He ignored "the rapidity with which events followed one another" and also "the influences that have been thrown about them."

Still another writer is of a commercial character, "inspired by the demand for sensational nonsense by the great newspapers of the East" which, shouted Mr. Freeman, "still find profit in stigmatizing this new Western country as abnormally wild and woolly in contra-distinction to the civilized and effete East."

Freeman was now beginning to warm up. "The Cattle King," he continued, "The Copper King, the Silver King, these and a dozen other titles are still forced upon the credulity of the uninformed to assist in throwing an air of mystery and awe about this bountifully endowed country." This was done in order "to strengthen the stories of fabulous wealth popularly supposed to be found beneath every rock and along every stream."

Freeman was prepared to admit that some few writers "studiously adhere to the path of truthfulness." But others, alas, assume that "truthfulness is the last element required." It was thus, he pointed out, that "the average mind is confused and clouded." And why not? "If the resources of the West are admitted, then the state of Western society is too unattractive. If large opportunities are conceded, it means a divorcement from all civilizing influences to grasp them." And so it continues: "Is the delightful healthfulness of our climate recognized? Then our weather is too rigorous. Our educational institutions are crude. Our religious life is stunted and warped. In short, a thousand things are lacking which are necessary, and another thousand are present which must be eliminated to make the West tenable . . . And thus doth the imagination today perform the functions that should rest with certain knowledge . . ."

Was it not pitiable? One can almost hear this stanch friend of the West cry aloud in his chagrin that in forty-five years of discovery, exploration and settlement, the "actual knowledge of conditions in the West had advanced almost not at all." Today, he observed, "a new West is being presented while the world is still wrestling with the traditions and legends of the old." And, mark you, "While the East is straining its eyes to catch a glimpse of evidence of a higher degree of civilization, the unsatisfied traveler is wearing himself out in vain search of lingering relics of primitive life."

Yet, was not all this and more a part of God's economy? "Logic," explained Freeman, "approves of the enveloping of true conditions in a certain mystery, to be dispelled only by slow stages of discovery and development in the working out for the whole nation of a destiny palpably intended for it."

There you had it, complete: God, Herbert Spencer, Manifest Destiny, and the United States of America, all rolled into one magnificent concept.

No longer is Freeman complaining. He is *telling* you: "Step by step have the borders of civilization been pushed from the banks of the Mississippi and the shores of the Pacific until they have merged into one. Gradually have the resources of the Western plains, valleys and mountains become the great producers of raw materials for the gigantic industries of the East."

And only now is Freeman ready for prophecy: "In due time will the industries of the East come creeping Westward to utilize these raw materials at the point of production. In their wake will come the people of a congesting East."

Freeman knows when all this will happen too: "It will all come in God's time . . . when an increasing vigor is vitally necessary . . . when the voice of power of a great nation in the events of the world needs be reinforced by the best manhood, by the highest industrial attainment, by the greatest material wealth, and by the broadest civilization . . ."

Here Philosopher Freeman reaches out for a few of his old friends, the Messrs. Darwin, Huxley, and Spencer: "What better school for development of the sturdiest men, to meet the strenuous struggle for supremacy of a whole nation, than the trials and hardships consequent upon the settlement of a great expanse like our West? It is the same school that will develop the youth of the present and coming generations. They shall stand as sponsors for the Republic's integrity for all time . . ."

Freeman is now ready for the climax: "They will go on, seeking out the dangers and the hardships until the East shall know no line of distinction . . . when the East shall be more Western and the West more Eastern . . . All honor to the West from whence beckoneth the star of empire to the youth of the East and the whole world—not to an empire where royalty reigns, but to a free country where brain and brawn are kings and where determination to *do* is a more priceless treasure than so much fine gold . . ."

I do not know that eloquent Harry Campbell Freeman ever read this nigh perfect Western essay aloud, at some Fourth of July or other celebration. It deserved reading aloud. And it deserved Sousa's Band, too, beating the very daylights out of "The Stars and Stripes Forever."

THE NORTHWEST CORNER (British Columbia—Washington—Oregon)

Chapter Two

Only recently the editor of a national magazine remarked that to the average Easterner, who has never been there, the Pacific Northwest is a vague and perhaps even mysterious place. He may, said this astute observer, be familiar with a few striking images, like the Columbia River and mountains named Hood and Rainier, with Puget Sound and the Olympic Peninsula; and, across the Canadian border, with Vancouver Island. Possibly he recalls pictures of skiing, salmon fishing, and a great deal of tall timber. Beyond that, all is downright mystery.

For this and other alleged reasons, the people who live in the Northwest often complain that they do not get the breaks in what has become known as "vacation literature," especially Back East. Those Easterners believe that the region is still pretty much the province of hunters and trappers, with a few hundred loggers lurking in the woods.

Although such notice is grossly exaggerated, due in part to the comparatively enormous traffic of tourists in California—

and with population gains there too—the Northwest has been filling up with what we might call settlers far too fast to suit many of us who liked it as it was before there were any dams on the Columbia River and before industrialists began putting up immense manufacturing plants that attracted even more tourists who only too often decided to stay and grow up with the country.

It is now 150 years since a young poet, William Cullen Bryant, wrote about the "continuous woods where rolls the Oregon, and hears no sound save his own dashings." He had never been within three thousand miles of the majestic stream he wrote about and seems not to have known it had even then been officially named and claimed as the Columbia River. This ignorance of the enormous country drained by the Columbia is typical of what in some degree prevails today. Yet the thought of the great lonely stream moved the young poet powerfully. He was right, too, in making it the first symbol of what was originally called simply the Oregon country and is now the Pacific Northwest.

Whether visitors come looking for hydroelectric power or electrifying scenery, the Columbia will do as the Northwest's first symbol, both American and Canadian. It has tributaries in seven states but the main stream rises in a small lake in British Columbia, little more than a pond that lies blue and cold and high on the roof of the continent, hemmed by the Rockies and the tumultuous Selkirks. I can think of no other place of geologic architecture more fitted to a headwaters than this complete drama of stone and glacier and water. This is Genesis, the fountainhead which starts the great surging stream on its tortured way a matter of more than twelve hundred miles to the sea in distant Oregon.

Though the headwaters lake is now available by car, comparatively few people have been there. I can't understand why, unless it is because few have heard of its glories. I'm a headwaters man myself, and that is just the place to begin looking at the Columbia. Up there, the Canadian portion of the stream is still primitive, still flowing through those "continuous woods" and filled with the very dashings Bryant heard in imagination,

460 miles of savage river before it crosses the forty-ninth parallel to enter the United States. But then it slows and deepens in the slack water behind Grand Coulee Dam. The river here has been tamed. From Grand Coulee to tidewater the Columbia has become a series of lakes and dams that supply power to all parts of the Northwest and also water to many irrigation projects.

The Columbia is the only stream that managed to hammer its way through the Cascade Mountains. Nowhere else, in this 750-mile-long range is there a passage. Through it went the covered wagons of the Oregon Trail, and through it today come many of the visitors by rail or highway. More important; the Cascades split the Northwest into two widely contrasting climates. The change is sudden. Even the slowly moving pioneers noticed it. For a thousand miles they had come through a region of light rainfall and sparse vegetation. The winter was cold, the summer blistering. As they came floating through these mountains, or followed along the Columbia's south bank, the sagebrush changed to trees of great girth; the sky turned to lead; mists swirled in little clouds around the headlands; and gentle rains began to fall. Meanwhile, they passed beyond the common range of magpies and rattlesnakes, beyond the fields of powdered lava, out of the land of terrible distances, and entered the biggest forest of big trees in North America.

The contrast remains. The Cascades mark two climates that can be seen, smelled, heard, and felt. There is a subtle yet noticeable difference in speech of natives; and even more difference in depth and shade of sun-and-wind tan. The range often divides political thought in Oregon-Washington; and occasionally, in times of stress, some embattled partisan is sure to propose that the Cascade Mountains ought of right to be the mutual border of four states, instead of running plumb down the middle of two.

Possibly because the United States is still a young country, we all of us have come to romanticize our pioneer and, as said, like to describe our region as the Last Frontier. The Northwest has a better than common claim to the distinction: It was the last corner of the United States to be settled. Although we had a trading post as early as 1813, the classic settler, who was the farmer-pioneer, did not arrive till the 1840s. It was a late start in disputed territory. Americans had to move fast to assure sovereignty at all, for the British Hudson's Bay Company had taken over John Jacob Astor's trading post, and opened a couple more before the covered wagons began to roll. The United States diplomats did well to extend their claims as far north as they did, at 49°.

The doubtful Oregon country was really won in little more than a decade. Things moved so rapidly that our pioneers hardly knew they were pioneers until somebody looked around to notice that shingles on the cabins had started to moss up. Then they organized a Society of Pioneers.

Meanwhile, generations have been born and reared in a vast country which, by and large, still defies the abilities of dedicated boosters to describe adequately. They have to deal, as intimated, with not one but two distinct regions, a fact little known elsewhere. Locally these are spoken of as east or west "of the mountains," meaning the Cascades. Though a visitor entering Idaho by train crossing the Snake River plains might consider that state no more than desert, he would be terribly wrong. Idaho is much a tumult of mountains. No railroad operates through it north and south. It contains the largest primitive area in the United States, a wilderness of wonders set aside by the federal government. It also contains, at Sun Valley, one of the fanciest and most luxurious recreation resorts imaginable. Much of the Idaho-Oregon border is the gorge of the Snake, rightly enough known as Hell's Canyon, said to be the deepest gash on the continent.

Eastern Oregon is a land of contrasts and complexities. In it are the well-publicized Wallowa Mountains, along with the lava beds of an immensity to give one to reflect on the convulsions that bred them; and the High Desert, a haunted country of infinite distances, of endless rimrock, marked by solitary buttes that are coal-black one moment, purple the next.

Bordering the deserts is the little-known Malheur Wildlife Refuge, some two hundred thousand acres to which come millions of astute birds who know a good thing, to rest and rear their young, then to take off for their other homes, the rare whooping cranes among them. Bordering the deserts in Idaho and eastern Washington and Oregon, in an astonishing pattern, are also the ponderosa pine forests, which range everywhere and provide a large part of the industrial income of the area.

Once the Cascades are crossed, the influence of the Japanese Current, a sort of Pacific Gulf Stream, becomes apparent. Western Oregon and Washington—and British Columbia—is often called the Evergreen Land. This is no fancy cooked up by chambers of commerce. It *is* green from January through December. Rain makes it so, and rain falls to the amount of 130 inches a year in the coastal strip, and inland to the top of the Cascades varies from some forty inches in the valleys to eighty inches in the higher elevations. And there, at the height of land, it virtually stops altogether.

Not long ago I was taken to task by eager professional boosters because I mentioned, in print, the "majestic gloom" of western Oregon, Washington, and British Columbia. Possibly "gloom" isn't just the right word, but I wanted to make it clear there are some people who like less glaring sunshine than is common east of the Cascades, who enjoy periods of lowering skies and vagrant mists which lend a touch of mystery to the landscape. If he wants more, all a man need do is to get into his car and drive an hour, or even three hours, eastward over the hump to find it, brilliant and lasting.

The greatest single natural feature west of the Cascades is the Douglas fir forest. It reaches from the California border up through Oregon, Washington, British Columbia into Alaska. From it, according to fairly reliable statistics, come sixty-five cents of every dollar that circulates in Oregon and Washington.

A great deal of the virgin timber stands in the several national forests and two national parks in the Northwest.

This endless forest harbors a variety of small and big game. The many streams that tumble down the west slope of the Cascades into the Columbia or the Willamette, or directly into the ocean, are well stocked with trout, steelhead, and salmon. Almost everybody, even those in the larger population centers, lives within shouting distance of both woods and water. Outdoor recreation areas are on the fringe of the towns and cities. The ski addict and the mountain climber never had it so good as here, what with peaks named Hood, Adams, St. Helens, Rainier, and Baker in his front yard. One of the most vivid impressions made on visitors is this nearness of urban dwellers to woods, streams, and mountains.

And to seashore. Oregon, Washington, and British Columbia front on more than a thousand miles of the Pacific. Much of the shore line is still in a wild or native condition. That the Coast Highway manages to follow it rather closely does credit to the engineers who laid it. This highway is not for those whose reason for travel is apparently to brag about mileage, but for those who like to look at what is exposed to their eyes. The same is true of the Olympic Peninsula, that Last Wilderness of the Rain Forest, whose northern front is the Strait of Juan de Fuca, across which one can see the tip of Vancouver Island, near which stands "the most English city" in America, Victoria, which began life as a sleepy trading post of the Hudson's Bay Company, and became the capital of British Columbia.

Another thing about the Olympia Peninsula: It is the place where residents can and often do refer to Seattle as "Back East," that metropolis being a little more than one hundred miles east of the busy logging town of Forks, Washington.

Then, there are the hundreds of miles of inland waterway called Puget Sound, threading Washington to Seattle, Tacoma, and Olympia, where the tiny oysters come from—and from nowhere else—and the superb spread of salt water named Hood Canal for a noted British admiral of the seas. It is not a canal at all, but an elongated inland sea on the shores of which are the melodiously named communities of Hamma Hamma, Humptulips, Lilliwaup, Dosewallips, Duckabush, and Quilcene. Poets have accomplished wonders with their names. Not even Maine or Michigan presents more opportunities.

No such virtuosity was expended in naming one of the Northwest's most engaging sights, which is Crater Lake. It is just that—a lake in a remnant of a volcano's casing. But what a lake! Until I saw it, I thought the intense blue it reflected from souvenir postcards and kodachrome photographs was the work of a master artist in the mixing of colored inks. But it is due, I'm told, to minerals and light. The government has seen fit to declare its uniqueness by forming Crater Lake National Park.

Like many a native, I am privately of the opinion that not only Crater Lake, and Mount Rainier, and the Olympics, and the Oregon Caves, and the Lava Beds should be in federal keeping, as they are, but that perhaps the whole Northwest should be set aside as one great park before it is wholly overrun by foreign immigrants like myself.

If as said, it pleases us in the Northwest to think of our particular corner as the Last Frontier, it is a harmless brag characteristic of the American West. Time has made of pioneers a romantic company sitting high in the Valhalla of national memory. But it is more accurate to say that we are in a new frontier period, that of the industrial frontier; and to say, too, that a considerable majority of the older residents dislike it. It has done havoc to their former easygoing way of life.

The industrial frontier arrived rather suddenly when the needs and emergencies of World War II created new and tremendous military installations and manufacturing plants accompanied by vast dispersions of populations. Almost exactly a century after the covered-wagon trains of the so-called Great Migration of Forty-three, several hundred thousand Americans came to work or train through the war period. Many of them have remained.

The end of the war did not bring a backwash. Instead, there

continued the movement of small industry from the east and midwest and south; of families seeking agricultural lands, including those reclaimed from the desert by the new irrigating facilities. During the decade after 1940, more than one million population was added to Oregon-Washington.

Scarcely a century separates the end of the fur trade and the Hanford Engineer Works, a nigh perfect euphemism for the plant, isolated in a desert along the Columbia River, which supplied some of the essences that went into the Hiroshima Bomb, and also into the first submarine vessel to operate by atomic power. One after the other the stern-wheeler, the stagecoach, the steam locomotive have gone over the hill, or over the falls, or to take their place in a museum.

The bewhiskered and footloose logger, yelling at his bull-team lurching down the skidroad or kicking the windows out of brothels and saloons, has become a smooth-faced young man with a family, and his major vice is cigarettes; he operates power machines. The old-time Indian fighter is now with Custer. The Indian himself buys salmon in cans, and if he wants firewater he is at liberty to buy it in a state liquor store. If his fathers lived on a timbered reservation, he may well buy Cadillacs today.

In this New Frontier period, even the scenery has been undergoing change, and among the best-selling Scenic Postcards is one with a simple legend: GRAND COULEE DAM, WASH., it says with stark brevity. This is of course the great federal project on the Columbia River. Begun in 1933, ten years later it went into partial operation, though the first irrigating water waited till 1952. For much of thirty years it has remained an outstanding favorite with tourists. This is so probably because there is nothing the average American tourist likes to see, and to prove he has seen, comparable to something Big, really BIG.

Grand Coulee Dam is big, certainly, but it has to contend with too much vacant space to *look* big. Set in the midst of appalling distances, it appears like a play dam for children, lost in the terrifying wastes that are now threaded with transmission lines. As center of the Northwest Power Pool, however, Grand

Coulee's influence is felt in all parts of the Northwest. If and when transmission of power is interrupted for any length of time, men may be laid off in the aluminum plants at Spokane, Tacoma, and Vancouver (Washington); and in the big sawmills, plywood mills, and pulp and paper plants of Port Angeles, Everett, Camas, and Longview, Washington; and Lebanon, Springfield, Medford, and Coos Bay, Oregon. It may well affect the operations of smelting and concentrating mills in the mining regions of Idaho. The shearing of sheep may be hampered on the far ranges. The canning of salmon at Astoria may be halted. What the regional press calls a critical "shortage of power" can make headlines all over.

Looking back no more than a century, one may ponder of the cultures that were brought here on the varied waves, some of them mere ripples, of immigration. The fur companies were officered by Scots and manned in large part by Canadian French or Indians. Many of the latter took native wives when they retired on farms in the Willamette Valley. They were Catholics, and missionary priests soon came to minister to them.

The first emigrants who came purposely to take up land were native Americans of so-called Anglo-Saxon stock, and in their vanguard were Methodist missionaries who founded the first college. The first hospitals were Catholic institutions. The "father of public education" in the old Oregon country was the Rev. George H. Atkinson, a Congregationalist from Massachusetts. Oregon Territory's first governor was Joseph Lane from North Carolina.

In the covered-wagon trains of the forties were many men who came simply because they had suddenly been taken with the newest fever of their kind, the Oregon Fever. Either they or their fathers had been through migrating fevers before. The urge had brought them first from the Atlantic Coast states to the Ohio country, next to Illinois, then to Missouri. It was a habit. In the process they had become virtually a class of professional pioneers; and they took to the Oregon Trail with little more thought of danger or hardships than if they were heading for some Fourth of July picnic or a camp meeting.

New Englanders were more likely to come by ship around the Horn, or across the Isthmus. Among them were many founders of Northwest towns and cities; of promoters of stage-coach, steamboat, and railroad lines; and always of schools and libraries. Emigrants born in Europe did not arrive in any great number until the transcontinentals came. By then Washington had been made into a territory and was about to be admitted to the Union. Germans seemed to favor Oregon. A majority of Scandinavians chose Puget Sound and Grays Harbor. Finns concentrated on Astoria. As elsewhere in the West, Chinese had been imported to build railroads, after which they followed the mining camps, then settled in colonies in Seattle and Portland. Japanese were scarce in the Northwest until well after the turn of the century. So were South Europeans.

For decades lumbering, fishing, and agriculture have been major occupations; and for decades little or no thought was given to the expendable nature of forests, the soil, and the fish. Year after year the Columbia was overfished with nets; with traps; with "Chinese lines" of multiple hooks, running to hundreds each; and with great salmon wheels, thirty feet in diameter, turned by the current day and night, which scooped all fish seeking to move upstream or down in customary channels and dumped them into a hopper, ready for the cannery. Both the wheels and the Chinese lines were eventually banned in the Northwest, and the taking of salmon was regulated by laws.

Farmers here as elsewhere were destined to try, and to be defeated by, the one-crop idea—usually grain—before they accepted the new religion of diversification; and many more discovered what is too often the fatal illusion of dry farming. Yet neither Oregon nor Washington quite became a dust-bowl problem, if only because several of the biggest irrigating projects in the United States helped to save them.

Though the over-all importance of forest products in the region has been cited, it should be stressed that when the logging operators arrived here, they had already cut a swath across the country clear from eastern Maine through the lake states, and also much of the South. Yet they still cherished the idea they had held for nigh three hundred years: There was always timber, plenty of timber, just over the next hump.

These hardy industrialists had never looked backward, eastward. Had they done so, the more reflective among them might have seen what was happening—that as fast as they abandoned their old works a horde of farmers, traders, and city promoters moved in to grub stumps, plat towns, and make highways of the grass-grown logging roads. It was the loggers' ancient enemy, Civilization, following hard in their wake, and they wanted none of it. They *got* it, of course, for here in the Northwest, loggers and lumbermen were in their last stronghold, their backs to the sea. And it was going to tame them too.

Conservation of timber, forestry, is too complicated a story to go into here. Let me say, however, that the tamed and long since "civilized" operators, working on the modern concept that timber is a crop, no longer leave cutover acres to the vagaries of fire, wind, and disease, but guard their second-growth lands as they would any other treasure, in enormous tree farms.

Thus the forest is still the incomparable source of livelihood in the Northwest. Oregon leads all states in the manufacture of forest products; Washington is in third place. (California is second.)

The three major cities in today's Northwest were founded on forest products, and so were scores of lesser towns in Oregon, Washington, and Idaho.

Seattle rises from the shore of Puget Sound and rambles up and over high hills. Its citizens like to call it the Gateway to Alaska because in 1898 it was the jumping-off port during the Gold Rush to the Klondike of that period. (Purists should know that the Klondike River is in Yukon Territory of Canada, not Alaska.) Seattle's setting is spectacular. In front is the sparkle of the Sound. At the city's back is Lake Washington. West across the Sound rise the jagged, glittering peaks of the Olympic

Mountains. To the city's north, east, and south loom the Cascades. Commanding all, when there is no mist, is the tremendous mass of Rainier—the Mountain—alone, aloof, majestic.

Seattle's character is simple and clear. It is the perennial boom town—gay and grim by turns, but always loud and lively, brassy and friendly; a backslapping place given to roaring, bragging Vision. There is perhaps no more hospitable city in the United States. In its Pioneer Square stands what is locally described as "the tallest totem pole in the world." Along its waterfront runs a major thoroughfare named Alaska Way. The city's position in relation to the short great-circle route to the Orient also gives it an advantage over other West Coast ports.

The Northwest's second city, Portland, is a deep-sea port more than a hundred miles from the ocean. Less spectacular than Seattle, its setting is dramatic enough, what with two big rivers flowing past or through the town and three major snow-capped peaks rising from the somberly beautiful Cascades. The older part of the city spreads west from the Willamette River, then mounts to the handsome semicircle of modest hills called The Heights. The city's east side is flanked by both the Willamette and the Columbia.

In character and atmosphere Portland is in contrast to Seattle. One of the oldest towns in all the American West, it was settled in some part by conservative New Englanders whose heritage is to be seen in the hundreds of acres of elm-shaded village green, a sort of Boston Common called the Park Blocks, inviolate these past hundred years. The pioneer Yankees also bequeathed attitudes and institutions, including a really great public library, a college, and an art museum which have had no little to do with the oft-quoted remark that Portland is the "Athens of the West." One of its two surviving newspapers, the *Oregonian,* observed its centennial back in 1950. Portland is one of the world's largest exporters of grain and forest products. It has long had close shipping ties with Hawaii and Japan.

The Northwest's third city, Spokane, rightly enough calls itself the Capital of the Inland Empire, a region embracing the rich Coeur d'Alenes and other mining districts; vast wheatlands and cattle ranges; and forests of white and ponderosa pines. Its rise was meteoric when the Northern Pacific came through and was followed by the Great Northern and the Milwaukee railroads, and by the Spokane International and a branch line of what is now the Union Pacific. This network of rails has given Spokane a commanding position as a marketing and distribution center for the intermountain country. Concentrated around the handsome falls of the Spokane River, the city has been spreading eastward over the level valley floor and southward over the rocky rim of low pine-covered hills.

How much of British Columbia's immensity should be considered within the usual orbit of American tourists is a matter of opinion. The orbit grows year after year, but it is safe to say it is still, in 1962, a very small portion of the province's 355,855 square miles.

Let us assume that most tourists are familiar with Vancouver Island from Victoria, the capital, to Alert Bay; and with the lower mainland around Vancouver, the largest city; and that others have crossed the province by the Canadian National Railway from Prince George; in Jasper National Park, to Prince Rupert; and a few have ridden the Pacific Great Eastern from Vancouver to Dawson Creek on the Alaska Highway.

My own approach to the American Northwest happened to be by way of British Columbia, where I lived for some three years. At that time, 1920–23, the stranger discovered, before he got to his hotel, that Vancouver was no Yankee town. His taxi ran on the left. So did other traffic, including the specially built streetcars. This was odd enough even in Canada, where otherwise, except for tiny Prince Edward Island off the East Coast, traffic followed the right-hand custom of the United States.

It was confusing at first, though one ceased to think of it; and it was fair notice to the outlander, either Canadian or American, that the Province of British Columbia proposed to live up to its name. This was a true *British* commonwealth. But there had been a mounting opposition to the left-hand rule. It presently congealed into a strong parliamentary clique and, after a good deal of impassioned oratory, the provincial legislators passed an act changing the rule of the road to right-hand. The time set for change was January 1, 1921.

Being still a resident of the province, I recall the uproar as the day drew near. The letter columns of the Vancouver *Province, Sun,* and *World,* and of the Victoria *Colonist,* were seething with bitter protests and denunciations regarding this un-British, even traitorous adoption of "Yankee notions." Various associations and societies were galvanized to action. They drew up and passed resolutions damning the whole business as the work of Satan in league with Uncle Sam. Letters signed John Bull and True Englishman were printed. What was good enough in the times of Gladstone, it appeared, what was good enough for the Pitts, both Elder and Younger, and doubtless, too, good enough for Beowulf, was good enough for British Columbia in the mid-twentieth century.

It was freely prophesied that collisions and wrecks would strew the streets and highways with carnage compared with which the field at Balaclava was as nothing. The awesome day came and passed. The local press reported that not a single accident occurred that could have been charged to the change.

It was a striking coincidence that on the same New Year's Day when the rule of the road was changed, the province also shook off the shackles of Prohibition and put into effect the government sale and control of liquor. It was the first political unit in North America, I believe, to adopt so sensible a law.

Vancouver was so new a city when I got there that almost nobody save children was a native of the place. Men hardly of middle age could recall the arrival of the first train of cars, which rolled into town on Queen Victoria's birthday, May 24, 1887, when Vancouver could muster less than two thousand population. The site had been chosen for the Canadian Pacific Railway's terminus by the line's general manager, William Van

Horne, and named for Captain George Vancouver, the English explorer who had mapped much of the Northwest coast and who already had a city named for him on the Columbia River in the state of Washington.

I thought when I first saw it, there was no other city anywhere with a more dramatic setting than that of Vancouver, British Columbia, and am still of that opinion. It was even then well on its way to becoming the third city in all Canada, the place it holds in 1962 (pop: 1956—365,844). It occupies a promontory on the mainland almost surrounded by water. Across the harbor to the north and east are great white-capped mountains. Five minutes' ride from the city center are the thousand acres of Stanley Park, all virgin forest to this day. On the edge of this superb primitive area of darkest green, Vancouver rises and glitters in the northern sunlight with a sparkle all its own. Mist and, in season, downright fog hang mysteriously over it. Snow is rare.

Whether or not the tendency in Vancouver and British Columbia has been toward "Americanization" these past forty years is debatable. It is still the most British of all the Canadian provinces, but nowhere except in the city of Victoria does there seem to be any conscious effort to keep it so. In Victoria is still a tweedy and sensible-shoed older population that firmly, and to my mind most properly, resists any effort at change. Working with them to this end are commercial interests that self-consciously keep Britishness alive to attract American tourists who enjoy scones and quaintness with their tea and are enchanted with Yule logs and policemen dressed like the bobbies of Old England. But cricket, which was in a thriving condition when I was first in the province, is now played virtually in private, even in Victoria. Vancouver has a baseball franchise in the Pacific Coast League, along with Seattle, Portland, and Spokane.

Vancouver is the most cosmopolitan city in Canada. Its Chinatown is the largest on the West Coast, after San Francisco's. One sees many turbaned East Indians, called Sikhs, on the streets, along with many westernized Japanese, and both mountain and tidewater native Indians. There are Seaforth Highlanders in white jackets and tartans, their kilts swaying. Added to the active military are more retired British army officers than you would readily believe. Almost without exception they appear to be at least colonels, who have taken their gin and bitters at Jodhpur, or Ladysmith, or Pretoria. They live largely in clubs, rooming houses, and "in chambers" all over town, and in small cottages in the outer suburbs. They carry canes and like bloaters for breakfast.

The venerable Hudson's Bay Company, operators of one of Vancouver's finest stores, has always been hospitable to men who have, as the saying used to be, served the Empire. Thirty years ago their employees would have included veterans of all of the Empire's wars from the Crimean to the one ending in 1918.

In the coastal country of the mainland, the Rockies come right down to the sea. There are no roads worth mentioning. Everything moves by ships which ply north to the Queen Charlotte Islands and around Vancouver Island. Logging and making lumber, including especially fine cedar shingles, are still a major industry. The region in and east of the Rockies is called the Interior. It is mountainous country devoted to mining, and in less degree to logging and the raising of fruits. Here, scattered throughout the orchard districts, are some fifteen thousand members of the Christian Community of Universal Brotherhood, Limited. These are the Dukhobors.

We in the States have had scores of strange sects, but nothing at all to compare to these fanatics. To all Americans, and to most Canadians, Dukhobors are known only as a crew of "foreigners" whose favorite amusements are the staging of nude parades, and arson committed on public schoolhouses. For many years they have been the periodic delight of the Sunday supplements of newspapers. Typical was a recent article that told how "several hundred naked Dukhobor men and women" led by a "raven-haired and nude young woman on a white horse" had swept through the British Columbia Interior, torches in hand, spreading fire in their wake. If you didn't believe the text, then you could gaze at a picture, a pen-and-ink-drawing of this "pretty Queen of the Dukhobors," her raven hair flowing like Lady Godiva's, astride the white steed, while in the rear came a riotous gang of men, women, and children, all stark naked, the men bearded, flaming torches in hand.

Although both text and picture were sheer fiction, the article was true in that it presented to the public what has long since been British Columbia's own conception of the sect. The raven-haired queen on the white horse was merely an added attraction in the best Sunday supplement tradition. Had she been a blond beauty, then her horse would have been "black as night," according to the strict rules of the Sunday supplement feature writers' union.

For half a century the Dukhobors have asked for and received the worst press imaginable. For this their leaders have been largely responsible. They have become one of British Columbia's greatest problems. The sect originated in a seventeenth-century schism in the Russian Orthodox Church. For the next two hundred years its adherents were shunted from one Russian province to another, beaten by Cossacks, robbed regularly by government agents, and imprisoned. Their great crime was that they refused to serve in the army. In time, they came to be vegetarians, non-drinkers of vodka, non-users of tobacco.

Near the turn of this century, Count Leo Tolstoy became interested in the sect. So did Aylmer Maude, an Englishman, and the Quakers. These people aided the Dukhobors to migrate to western Canada. Ten thousand came in 1899 to settle homesteads in what is now Saskatchewan. Later their leader, Peter Veregin, who had spent many years in Siberian exile, was permitted to join his people. They called him Peter the Lordly. I saw him once in a small hotel in Winnipeg. He was big, bearded, and the papers said he looked much like his mentor Tolstoy.

Peter was an able and crafty leader. He publicly deplored

the mass nudism and other didoes of the inner sect, called the Sons of Freedom, and encouraged them privately in their antipathy to public schools. The Sons staged parades of protest whenever the spirit moved them. When World War I came, the Canadian government had its hands full. Though the entire sect had been expressly exempted from military duty, most of them refused to sign for their homestead deeds, because they must also swear allegiance to the Crown. They were dispossessed, and Peter led a majority of them to British Columbia, where they purchased land in the name of their corporation, the aforesaid Christian Community of Universal Brotherhood, Limited.

At Brilliant, B.C., the hard-working group started raising fruit. They put up a big jam factory. Their products were noted for high quality, and for a time they prospered. They built a large sawmill and waterworks. This was too much progress for the inner-sect Sons of Freedom. They broke away and set up a village of their own, a grim place they named Krestova. The first public schoolhouse in the Dukhobor district was destroyed by fire in 1923. Some eighty more have been burned since. Then came the event beside which all others in Dukhobor history paled.

On the evening of October 28, 1924, Peter the Lordly boarded a Canadian Pacific train at Brilliant. With him was a Dukhobor woman. The pair had tickets to Grand Forks, a hundred miles farther on. The train never got there. Near the hamlet of Farron it was stopped by a mighty blast that tore the day coach into splinters and twisted steel. Peter was killed. So was the Dukhobor maid and seven other passengers. The mystery was never solved.

Peter's death marked the beginning of the slow disintegration of the Dukhobors. His son, who became leader, was given to the bottle, and seemingly worked to undermine the spirit and economy of his people. This is the opinion of J. F. C. Wright, Canadian journalist and writer whose *Slava Bohu,* published in 1940, is a sound and fascinating study of this strange sect. In any

2. British Columbia was the first landfall I made when I first came west of the Rockies. This is the entrance to Lion's Gate Bridge, Vancouver.

3. Between Seattle and Portland, in the somberly beautiful Cascades, you come to Spirit Lake and Mount St. Helens. Peak is 9671 feet high.

4. Oregon, Washington, and British Columbia front on more than a thousand miles of the Pacific. Much of the shore line is still in a wild or native condition. (*Heceta Head, Oregon*)

5. The hundreds of miles of inland waterway called Puget Sound thread through Washington to Seattle, Tacoma, and Olympia, where the tiny oysters come from.

6. In the coastal country of British Columbia's mainland, the Rockies come right down to the sea. There are no roads worth mentioning. Everything moves by ship. (*Horseshoe Bay, West Vancouver*)

7. If it pleases us in the Northwest to think of our particular corner as the Last Frontier, it is a harmless brag characteristic of the American West. (*Glacier Lake, Northeastern Oregon*)

8. Of the three northwestern states, Idaho seems to have had what may be called the purest "western" history: in one bound it went from Beaver to Gold. (*Silver City, Idaho, Once Thriving Gold Mining Town*)

9. The 750-mile-long range of Cascade Mountains splits the Northwest into two widely contrasting climates that can be seen, smelled, heard, and felt. (*Mount Adams, Washington, in the Cascade Range*)

10. Almost 40 per cent of Idaho is still in forest land, and 36 per cent of this is still in government ownership, in the national forests. (*Bitterroot Mountains, Idaho*)

event, they buried Peter the Lordly in a tomb of rock high on a mountain near his old headquarters at Brilliant. It has since been dynamited half a dozen times by unknown parties.

Compared to the American Northwest, British Columbia has scarcely begun to exploit its natural resources. The visiting tourist seldom appreciates its vastness. Let no Texan go there to brag of the size of his own great state. It would be wholly swallowed by British Columbia and leave almost no trace. I found it as delightful a country as man could live in. It had and still has gorgeous scenery. Life was not too hard. People lived calmly. The pace everywhere, town or country, was leisurely. The people had their own ways and customs, and, they held fast to these. I have reason to believe that this is no longer true. People and province have been caught in the heady current called Progress. Anything new is wonderful. Anything old is to be deplored.

I can see nothing to prevent British Columbia from becoming the great hive of population and of industry and commerce that a majority of its citizens seem to want. Only yesterday there were, in all its immensity, only half a million people, only a few more than are now living in greater Vancouver alone.

Prophets of Progress in a region so rich in natural resources as British Columbia are to be listened to. In another decade, perhaps, the current crop of seers may well be valued because, back in the 1960s, they were trying to *warn* of costs that accompany the booming times of Progress.

It has been forgotten that at one time British Columbia seemed destined to vote itself into the Union of the United States. The province was so isolated by the Rocky Mountains from the rest of the new Dominion of Canada, that much of its commerce and even its communications were carried on with or through the neighboring states of Washington, Idaho, and Montana. Either that, or by sea when the nearest port was distant Montreal.

Thus a railroad from Ottawa, the Dominion's capital, was

needed; and it was started, to crawl west so slowly at first that the Crown Colony of British Columbia tired of waiting and its primitive local government met to consider joining the United States. The vote indicated a strong though not quite a majority wish to take so radical a step. The vote was probably more a resentment against the Dominion Government than it was a genuine desire to merge with its old enemy. In any case, it was effective. To make certain no such hideous thing should ever happen, Canada's Prime Minister, John A. Macdonald, promised that the Canadian Pacific should be pushed through the Rockies as fast as possible, to bind the long-isolated province to the Dominion.

The official Last Spike was driven near Revelstoke, B.C., on November 7, 1885. The Dominion had been spanned. Old Montreal and new Vancouver were connected by rails. By that time, the boundary between Canada and the United States had officially been settled by the Webster-Ashburton Treaty of 1842.

But there remained a lot of unfinished local business in the American Northwest, as Washington, Idaho, Montana, and Wyoming were carved out of the original Territory of Oregon.

THE NORTHWEST CORNER (Washington—Oregon—Idaho)

Chapter Three

Modern history began happening in the Northwest Corner on the cloudy morning of May 11, 1792, when the brig *Columbia,* Captain Robert Gray, out of Boston, came plunging full sail over a foaming white bar that had attracted the skipper's attention while he was cruising the West Coast for furs.

Captain Gray appears to have been the laconic type of Yankee. Three lines in his log serve to bring the ship over the terrible bar, and into a stream he judged to be a good ten miles wide near its mouth. Some six lines are devoted to soundings and bearings, one line to pumping out the casks and filling them from the stream. Then, "So ends," he wrote. He might better have written it, "So begins," for the story of the great river begins with Gray.

A day or so later Gray bethought himself to declare this to be Columbia's River, then went to trading with the natives, large numbers of whom came in canoes to the vessel. From among them he got 160 prime sea-otter skins, worth up to $100 each in China. Then he sailed promptly out of the stream and virtually out of history; but he had discovered, named, and claimed the long sought River of the West and thus obliterated the apocryphal Northwest Passage.

Then, in 1803, the United States made the Louisiana Purchase, and soon after came the first official party to explore the vast new region, the Lewis and Clark Expedition. In October 1805 Lewis and Clark first laid eyes on the great surging stream that had been flowing in and out of men's imaginations for many years; and by November 7 they camped where they could see, between the receding banks of the river, the bright expanse of the Pacific. "Ocian in view," Clark wrote in his journal. "O, the joy!" The waves of the Great South Sea were coming in from China.

More than a century and a half later, the expedition's importance in United States history is still in process of interpretation. Some writers tend to credit it alone for acquisition of the Oregon country, which was not a part of the Louisiana Purchase and was, at best, of doubtful sovereignty. Granting that the expedition was of paramount importance in regard to Oregon, the late Bernard DeVoto believed its greatest contribution was that it gave the entire West to the American people as "something the mind could deal with."

Before, this void had been a region of rumor, guess, and fantasy. But Lewis and Clark peopled the unknown with specific tribes of Indians, named its flora and fauna, mapped its mountains and rivers, described the varying climates, and dissipated forever the ancient myth of a Northwest Passage. After Lewis and Clark, the mind could focus on reality. And it did: Only five years later an American trading post had been established near the mouth of the Columbia, and a supporting party was making its way overland from St. Louis.

With the Louisiana Purchase began the territorial growth of the United States beyond the Mississippi. Later additions included the annexation of Texas (1845), that of the Oregon country (1846), and the so-called Mexican Cession (1848). Meanwhile, the Webster-Ashburton Treaty (1842) had seemed to settle the question of the boundary between the United States and Canada. So, periodically, the new trans-Mississippi lands were organized formally into territories, then states of the Union. Here in the Northwest, for example, Oregon Territory included what became the states of Oregon, Washington, Idaho, and parts of Montana and Wyoming.

It has been said that the original Oregon country has the distinction of being the only region added to the United States by three different means, none of them military—discovery, exploration, and occupation. This is true, but it was not accomplished without a struggle accompanied, briefly, by a lot of belligerent talk, sparked by the alliterative American demand of "Fifty-four-forty or fight," which had to do with longitude during the joint occupancy of Oregon by British and American interests.

Almost simultaneously, the minds of both British and Americans began to focus on realities. In the same year Lewis and Clark came down the lower Columbia, men of the Northwest Company of Montreal, fur traders, came over the Canadian Rockies and set about exploring rivers and establishing posts. And by 1811 one of these men, David Thompson, who had already found the source of the Columbia, shoved off to follow that stream to its mouth.

It was a hardy voyage, during which Thompson and his paddlers wore out three canoes. They paused while Thompson posted a notice by which he claimed the region for Great Britain, adding that the Northwest Company of Canada planned to "erect a factory at this place for the Commerce of the Country around." But when the doughty Briton arrived at what is now Astoria, Oregon, he was dismayed to find a stockaded compound over which flew the American flag. It was a spearhead of John Jacob Astor's plan to make his American Fur Company into a trading monopoly of North America.

Disguising both his surprise and disappointment, Thompson gave Astor's men to understand they would waste their time should they attempt to erect posts east of the Cascade Mountains. Why, said he, his own outfit had found the interior to be barren of furs. Then, after "civil entertainment," he took off up-river, followed by a party of Astorians just to make sure Thompson did not secure all the good interior locations.

Astor's plan was as bold as it was feasible, and fully as dangerous: He would plant at the Columbia's mouth a central establishment, with subordinate posts through the Northwest. The furs would thus be gathered at the point nearest to their sources, and nearest also to the richest market, or China. Having disposed of the furs, Astor's vessels were to reload with spices for the United States and return to New York. It looked pretty good.

But the War of 1812 interfered. In the face of reports that British men-of-war were already in the Pacific, Fort Astoria was sold to the Northwest Company of Canada. HMS *Racoon* entered the Columbia to take possession; and as new Fort George the post opened for business. At war's end, the Treaty of Ghent declared that all territory, places, and possessions taken by either party from the other should be restored. Fort George was returned to the United States. Astor decided not to resume operations, and the Canadian company was permitted to continue. A convention of joint occupancy was entered into by the two nations.

The Northwest Company Post at Astoria was soon taken over by its ancient competitor, the Hudson's Bay Company, an outfit whose policy indicated a dogmatic belief in the permanence of the British Empire. For more than a century and a half it had seen trading concerns come and go. It was patient with the wisdom of ages. It seemed also to be as relentless as time, and its governor and gentlemen adventurers were no men to desert the Empire in time of need.

And so, presently to Astoria came George Simpson, soon to be knighted, and with him Dr. John McLoughlin, whom Simpson had recently promoted to the Bay Company's chief factor, to consider matters in this, their new western department. At a spot on the Columbia opposite present Portland, they established what was to be the Bay's headquarters in the Oregon Country, with McLoughlin in charge, and christened it Fort Vancouver.

The location of this imposing post had been chosen with some care. It was the natural starting point for parties going south up the Willamette River or overland to Puget Sound. Governor Simpson believed that although nothing could stop American settlers from going anywhere in the Oregon country, he directed factor McLoughlin to steer them as far as possible to lands south of the Columbia.

Simpson was right. On came the Yankee settlers. Fur traders, fish packers, missionaries, families seeking farms. One and all they called to see Dr. McLoughlin, who was kind, courteous, yet persuasive in urging them to settle south of the Columbia in the Willamette Valley. One of the missionaries, the Reverend Jason Lee, opened a school for Indians, then turned his talents to politics. Making the rounds of the scattered settlers, almost half of whom were retired veterans of the Bay Company's trap lines, he got signatures to a petition asking Congress to provide a territorial government for Oregon, which he sent to Washington. When nothing came of it, Lee left on foot overland to the Atlantic Coast, and in person presented a second petition to Congress. Then he went about recruiting more settlers.

In May 1840 Lee returned by ship to the Columbia, with him a party of fifty-one new settlers whom Lee's compelling eloquence had shaken from their native homes. This party went into Oregon history, with capitals, as the Great Enforcement. When later a settler died intestate, the settlers held a meeting "with probate powers." They elected justices of the peace and four constables, and named a committee to frame a constitution and draft a legal code. This was the first of several get-togethers out of which came a provisional government that was to last from 1846 until Oregon Territory was formed two years later.

Dr. McLoughlin could not contain the Americans south of the Columbia. They continued to move north, to settle on the Cowlitz River and Puget Sound. Then, in 1843 and again in 1845, came really great migrations which, combined, brought some four thousand American settlers, to rut the Oregon Trail so deep it could be seen a century afterward; and to make of the Covered Wagon a symbol fit to join the *Mayflower* in the legendry of America. The ship of the great plains, the prairie schooner, was on its way into song and folklore.

Until the very last of the Covered Wagon people had crossed the plains, they remembered the biggest sun and the biggest moon in the biggest skies they had ever seen. It was the hottest sun, the coldest moon. Mirages danced ahead of their wagons, or flickered in their wake; and the youngsters cried with joy, then wept bitterly as a handsome blue lake suddenly appeared, shimmering cold and inviting for a few moments, then sank out of sight into the horizon. It came to seem as if their goal and the horizon were moving in unison; they were not getting anywhere. The wind never ceased. It blew straight out of hell, then from the antipodes. It piled up dark murk that split in thunderous crashes, and out of it came salvos of cast-iron hailstones, to stun the imagination and to fell oxen in their yokes.

The sun was worse than the wind. Here in the great void there was no getting away from the sun. You could not hide from it. Worse was its confusing brightness. A gopher was seen plainly to be a coyote, a clump of sagebrush became a mounted Indian; a wrecked and abandoned wagon grew and grew until it loomed like a monstrous barn, then fused with nothingness . . . But on went the wagons, and out of the wagons—when desperate men saw that Time was passing them, that they must mend their pace lest they be caught in a mountain winter—out of the great wagons went a massive bureau of carved oak, or a chest, a chair or two, or even an organ. Winter must not find families on the trail; out went the furniture.

Parkman the historian saw the furniture strewn along the trail that led to Oregon. He recognized, as did lesser men, that these things were not the mere trumpery of households, but were the last physical evidence of family status or at least of family continuity. They were not discarded lightly. Next to food and powder, they were the last things to be left along the way. A family who jettisoned them was a family in desperate straits.

These were among the things talked or thought about in later years, when the pioneers gathered for reunions and remembered their youth in the circle of campfires blinking like small red eyes in the endless dark.

The Great Migration of Forty-three astonished and dismayed the Hudson's Bay Company, and also the British Government. The grasping Americans were demanding all of the Pacific Northwest. Congress served notice of the end of the so-called joint occupancy. Great Britain, however, proposed a compromise to relinquish its claim to all land south of the forty-ninth parallel, provided the United States would give up its claim to land north of that line. The offer was accepted. War was averted. By this time the Hudson's Bay Company was moving out of Oregon, to set up new headquarters in British Columbia.

The Oregon country had not yet been organized as a territory of the United States, but an event of violence hastened legislation to make it so. This was the Whitman Massacre in the Walla Walla region of present Washington, when Marcus Whitman and his wife Narcissa, missionaries, together with twelve of their people, were murdered by Cayuse Indians. The provisional government of Oregon raised and armed five hundred men to run down the guilty braves, five of whom were later hanged. In Congress the Oregon Bill was hastily passed and signed by President James K. Polk, who appointed General Joseph Lane territorial governor. In 1853, those settlers who had taken lands north of the Columbia petitioned for separation from Oregon under style of Territory of Columbia, though the new subdivision was designated Washington Territory; from this new unit came Idaho Territory which, in turn, contributed lands toward the forming of Montana and Wyoming.

Oregon gained statehood in 1859, Washington in 1889, Idaho in 1890. These three states, as said earlier, comprise the American Pacific Northwest.

If state lines followed topography, instead of political needs, those small pieces of western Montana and Wyoming which are in the Columbia River drainage, by reason of the Kootenai and Snake rivers, would have remained in Idaho. But let us leave those two vast states for consideration later.

Of the three northwestern states, Idaho seems to have had what may be called the purest "western" history: in one bound it went from beaver to gold. In another bound from gold to bona fide settlers, with schoolhouse and an irrigation canal three miles long. These events were accompanied by an almost continuous war between trappers and Indians, between gold rushers and Indians, and lastly between the desperate red men and soldiers of the United States Army.

First of all, of course, as elsewhere in the northern part of the Rocky Mountain region, came Lewis and Clark, who crossed and recrossed both Idaho and Montana on their way to and from the Oregon country. One Idaho historian observed that though these explorers "found fur-bearing animals so thick they were in one another's way," the fur companies did not follow at once. Military posts had to be built first along the explored routes and "a good many Indians had to be killed or bribed or driven out . . ."

The first fort in present Idaho was Kullyspell House, built near Lake Pend Oreille by David Thompson then of the (British) Northwest Company, later merged with the Hudson's Bay outfit to become for many years a monopoly from Puget Sound to the headwaters of the Missouri. The Bay Company established Fort Boise, and later bought Fort Hall, built by Andrew Wyeth. Until abandoned in 1855, Fort Hall was a sort of wayside inn for the wagon trains, and also for stray trappers, missionaries, priests, Indians, gold seekers, and nondescript adventurers both within and outside the law.

A monument today commemorates the site of Fort Hall, and rightly enough. Emigrants coming out of the lonely deserts eastward could "see from afar its cool whitewashed walls, its red flag lettered H.B.C., and once within its walls, they could forget for a while the vast empty landscapes out of which they had come."

Trappers were still moving here and there in the mountains in 1860, though the great demand for beaver had long since passed, and gold was discovered in the Clearwater country of present Idaho. The first strike was made in March by Captain E. D. Pierce, a trader, and five men on a small creek which, because of the fine quality of the gold, the prospectors named Orofino. Before snow had melted, three hundred miners had appeared as if from nowhere and gone to work. A month more, and the Orofino diggings on the Clearwater River were swarming with a thousand newer arrivals. News of the find was now loose in distant Portland, and the Oregon Steam Navigation Company there met the challenge by laying out a town, Lewiston, at the mouth of the Clearwater.

This happened to be in violation of a treaty with the Nez Perces, but nobody seemed to mind, and the Navigation Company started hauling freight at $40 a ton, and passengers at $60 a fare. A little steamer took in $18,000 a trip, while also clearing profits of $600 at the bar. By mid-1861, the new town of Lewiston had 3000 inhabitants. By early fall, camps on the Clearwater were shipping $100,000 a month in gold to Portland, and prospectors had moved to another branch of the Snake River, the Salmon, and were testing the bars for a hundred miles south.

The gang on the Salmon failed to find anything, and were about to seek a short cut back to the Clearwater, when one of them "found about five cents worth of gold at the roots of a tree." He dug on a while, then washed out a dollar value. His comrades came to look. Within a few days, it was obvious that the Salmon was richer than the Clearwater. In March 1862 there was a veritable stampede from Portland to the Salmon River diggings.

But even richer things were in store for Idaho. Prospectors

were pushing south of the Salmon into the Boise Basin. They were ranging north into the Panhandle. Bancroft the historian saw them as like quicksilver. They dropped into any locality, "then broke up into individual globules and ran off in any direction, seeking any atom of gold in the vicinity." They stayed no longer than the gold attracted them. Notwithstanding their early regulations against Chinese working in the mines, when the Nez Perce diggings had yielded up their richest deposits these more patient toilers were permitted to take what remained by paying six dollars a month tax.[1]

The Boise Basin, drained by the creeks that flowed south into the Boise River, turned out to be the richest small gold placer ever discovered in the Northwest. By 1880 it had produced $250 million. The town of Boise was destined to be the state's capital, though Lewiston was the first capital of Idaho Territory, which came into being in 1863. In that year the Army built Fort Boise, overlooking Boise City, and this marked the end of trouble between the Indians and the miners. But not among the miners themselves. Nor among the sheep and the cattlemen.

Cattle came first, arriving in herds from Utah and Wyoming, and for a while Idaho was a huge cattle ranch. Thousands of beef were driven East to Cheyenne and shipped before the railroads came—and sheep with them—and another war was on. Dead sheepherders were often found in lonely spots along the barbed wire. Cowhands were ambushed. Now and then gangs of masked men, armed with wire cutters, appeared along the fences; and the open range was again open, if only briefly. The barbed wire eventually won, as it did elsewhere.

As the nineteenth century went into its last decade, Idaho in 1890 became a state, the forty-third in the Union, and the century closed in the middle of the biggest mining excitement of all. Gold and silver were discovered in the Coeur d'Alene re-

[1] Many years later, in the old Fraser River diggings of British Columbia, I was fascinated to watch Chinese working the tailings, piled on the river banks as long ago as the 1850s, and wondered how things were panning out. Naturally, I never learned, but Chinese are not given to wasting time.

gion. This time, the railroads had reached into Idaho. It wasn't long till mining became a corporate enterprise, but it still could not be called an orderly business. The mine owners were aggressive fellows. The miners themselves turned out to be pretty tough, too, and for a decade the Coeur d'Alene district was synonymous with trouble.

Dynamite was the new and terrible weapon. Miners and mines and mills were victims, and the violences culminated on December 30, 1905, when Frank Steunenberg, former Governor of Idaho, was blown to bits by a set bomb waiting at the gate of his home in Caldwell. This murder became a *cause célèbre.* It resulted in the making of three national heroes, or villains, depending on where you were standing. They were William E. Borah, Senator from Idaho; Clarence Darrow, attorney; and William D. (Big Bill) Haywood, a leader of the Miners Union and of the I.W.W., the Industrial Workers of the World. The man who set the bomb, Harry Orchard, served forty-nine years in the Idaho penitentiary, and died forgotten in 1954. By that time Idaho had long since emerged from its frontier period. That its formative days were as wildly violent as those of any other western state seems probable.

Far away, and long ago. Yet to me, and to many another, Idaho happily, almost magically, retains a flavor of its past. It stands as the forty-second state in rank so far as population is concerned. In all its 84,000 square miles there were but 662,000 heads to be counted in 1958. Of its over-all area, almost 40 per cent is still in forest land. And of this immense total, 36 per cent is still in government ownership, in the national forests. These range from the Sawtooth, the Bannock and Cache on the borders of Nevada and Utah, to the Kaniksu facing British Columbia. The Yellowstone and Grand Teton National Parks virtually border on Idaho, though they are in Wyoming; and Glacier National Park is nearby in Montana.

When in the 1950s, Muriel Sibell Wolle, historian-artist, came to Idaho, working on her classic, *The Bonanza Trail,* she was thrilled to find that the state "from top to bottom is full of mining camps, most of them fairly accessible." Only a very few were to be reached only by trails.

What Mrs. Wolle was doing, over several years, was running down all of the old mining camps in twelve western states, visiting to sketch them, even when little save the site remained; and writing short histories of their rise and fall. Two fine and immense volumes were the result.[2] That so sophisticated a mine-camp woman should have found Idaho a happy hunting ground as late as 1953 means that there must indeed have been a great many of them to begin with; and that the Idaho climate, like so much of the intermountain region, is kind to the longevity of wood structures.

It is not too much to say that mine towns are among Idaho's most popular Tourist Attractions. Numbers of them are still as active as in their heyday. Others may have faded somewhat, yet are supported by at least one deep ledge where the mixed veins contain enough gold, silver, galena, lead, and whatever to warrant continued working. Then there are many famous old camps which seemingly have no visible means of support, where empty structures tell of former saloons, stores, Miners Union Halls, Masonic halls, post offices, railroad stations, churches, schools, and other conveniences to present nostalgia that is mellow or grim or sad or merely the disordered remains of towns and cities in which at some time or other lived anywhere from five hundred to ten thousand people, man, woman, and child.

I happen to believe that Idaho has not made as much of its mine towns, ghost or otherwise, as attractions for visitors, as is warranted by their large number and availability. They begin on the north with the old camps of the Coeur d'Alene region, which include Eagle City, Wallace, Wardner, Kellogg, Mullan, Murray, Burke, and Gem; then into Lewiston, the district of

[2] *Stampede to Timberline, The Ghost Towns and Mining Camps of Colorado,* Published by the Author, 763 Sixteenth Street, Boulder, Colo.; and *The Bonanza Trail, Ghost Towns and Mining Camps of the West;* Indiana University Press, Bloomington, 1953.

Orofino and Pierce; south again to the Salmon River, where notable strikes were made at Elk City, Florence, and Salmon; still south into the Boise region, to take in Quartzburg, Pioneerville, Centerville, Placerville, and Idaho City; and at last the satellites of Silver City in the southwest corner of the state, which included places named DeLamar, Dewey, and Ruby City.

Let the visitor drive almost where he will in the northern, middle, or southern diggings, he is certain to come soon or late to one or more of the old mine camps in the state of Idaho, a Shoshoni word, often interpreted as meaning "Gem of the Mountains," hence the Gem State.

Although Idaho's popular nickname has nothing to do with gems as such, but appears to be a free-wheeling translation of the Shoshoni exclamation meaning, "Behold the sun coming down the mountain!" the state is rich with semiprecious stones, often of unusual quality, and the tourist season attracts large numbers of rock hounds.

Agate, jasper, and opal are found in the lava flows of south Idaho. Sapphires, rubies, and garnets are in the central and western regions. Opals of gem fineness are in the lava flows of the Panhandle. Within a mile of Boise, the state capital, is jasper, ranging in color through green, red, and purple. The western section of Owyhee County yields jasper together with agates of various types and colors. Here, too, are two-toned green quartz plasma, fine clear rock crystals, and agatized wood. From one opal mine along the Snake River were taken 7000 carats in the rough. In Gem County are lovely fire opals in the lava of Squaw Butte, near Emmett, and nearby are fine water agates of pale blue.

Near Weiser, Washington County, is a large deposit of silicified wood of bright yellow color that looks like natural oak; it is hard, free from flaws, and takes striking luster with polishing. Adams County has sapphires, rubies, and fine pink garnets near New Meadows. Flawless blood-red rubies have been found here that weighed two carats after cutting and polishing. In about the center of the state, between the Salmon and Lost rivers, is what many rock hunters call paradise. Cluttered over the entire area are agates of every sort—red, yellow, and green. Jasper is abundant. At Challis is a deposit of rich black limestone containing coral that takes a high white polish. South of here are said to be the best specimens of mordenite known.

There is amethyst near Hailey; opals and opalized wood in Lincoln and Gooding counties; fire opal near Moscow; and a big White Bird fossil deposit in Idaho County where maple leaves fourteen inches in diameter have been found.

As in Oregon and Washington, lumber and wood products are Idaho's first industry. Both technology and conservation have kept up with practices in the two larger states; but in Idaho one of the biggest sawmills in the world has found it good to continue the ancient and classic method of moving its trees from the stump to the millpond. This is the log drive down the Clearwater River.

The Clearwater drive of Potlatch Forests is not only the biggest drive in the United States, but one of the last. Elsewhere, east, west, and south, the diesel truck and a few diesel locomotives move the logs from woods to mill. Possibly the Clearwater drive is by now unique. At least I know of no other drive of *long* logs anywhere in the country—and a piddling few of pulpwood.

Driving logs down rivers is the most dramatic scene I know of in modern industry. That it is still to be witnessed once a year in Idaho seems as incredible as would any other antique practice long since discarded. Potlatch Forests, however, is no concern to indulge in antiquities for the sake of old-time flavor. It is one of the outstandingly modern operations of the vast Weyerhaeuser interests of St. Paul, Minnesota; and the drive has proved the most efficient method of bringing logs to its great mill on the Clearwater. No visitor to Idaho in season should miss it.

The summer I last saw it, the catfooted men of Potlatch drove eighty million board feet of big and long white-pine logs a distance of 120 miles, from headquarters camp to the booms at

Lewiston. Stan Profitt, a veteran of this and other streams was boss of the Clearwater drive. With the water running high and wild, and the logs ahead of them, Stan and forty drivers set out in late April with their two wanigans, noble craft, each 24 by 84 feet, perfect for the Clearwater.

On one was the cookhouse and dining room, plus the cook's quarters. On the other were double-decked bunks. These wanigan rafts were built of cedar logs, light as cork, bound crosswise with wild-cherry poles, the poles kept in place with tough elastic saplings of cherry pegged into auger holes.

The shelters on the rafts were frame and canvas, with all furniture bolted into place to withstand the rocking and heaving that goes with shooting the white waters of the Upper Clearwater. At each end of each raft was a big sweep, fifty feet long, with a sixteen-foot blade. These were manned by strong men under direction of pilot Bill Atkins, a river mariner.

Bill brought this lumberjack navy safely through the rough going near McKinnon's Cabin and Jump-Off-Joe Riffles. Many times water surged up over the deck and into the cookhouse, but never high enough to douse the fire in cook Bill Coons's stove, a stove, by the way, that was fed with small, round Presto logs, a product of the Potlatch mills, and made from what used to be called sawmill waste.

For a part of the drive one other craft joined the navy. It carried two caterpillar tractors, something I had never seen before on a river drive. They came into use soon enough, to aid in breaking jams and for moving single logs off shoals and rocks and out of eddies. The rafts transported the big tractors through stretches where they could not travel along the river banks.

Spring that year brought exceptionally high water. Fewer logs than usual hung up, but the flood turned Little Canyon into a roaring chaos of rapids that no craft could navigate. So, for five days the wanigans were tied up at the mouth of the Little Canyon, waiting till the high waters should abate somewhat; and, for the first time in Clearwater driving history, the whole crew moved into the Helgeson Hotel at Orofino, taking it over lock, stock, and parlor, to live like lords.

On June 2, the river level dropped, and the wanigans cast off and went shooting down Little Canyon. It was an exciting run, made quickly and safely, for pilot Atkins and his crew manned the sweeps deftly; the wanigans never got out of the channel. Late that day the whole shebang entered the broad stream of the main river.

From here on the going was fine, compared to the upper stream. Logs jammed now and then, of course, but men in bateaux, the classic boats of drivers, time out of mind, were quick to break them up. Several times the cats were brought into use, and proved their worth. Resort to dynamite was made once to start a jam moving. Mostly, however, it was skillful work with peavey and pike pole that jogged the sticks and sent them on their way.

The wanigans kept pace with the crew, tying up at strategic places for the night. Evening found most if not all of the crew at the wanigans. They had eaten four meals since arising. Eight hours on and in the water make a man ready for his bunk; but before going to bed every man jack took care of his calked boots. If the sharp calks had been blunted, they were removed with a chisel, the holes filled with little pegs of pine, then new calks driven into the wood.

Every night the drivers rinsed their shoes and hung them on the handles of peaveys stuck into the raft. Before breakfast most of the old-timers filled their shoes with water and let them soak during the meal, just as I had seen veterans do in Maine and on the Connecticut River in times past.

Sixty-two days were required to take the eighty million board feet from the landings on the upper stream and put them into the booms at Lewiston. A week later most of the drivers were back in the Potlatch woods, turned loggers again. The Clearwater was quiet again. The drive had gone down.

CALIFORNIA, THE MIRACLE

Chapter Four

The discovery of gold in California, early in 1848, was generally described at the time as due to an accident; James W. Marshall was not a prospector; he was digging a millrace.

But the results of his find have been so astonishing as to seem miraculous, and for more than a century good Californians have often credited the discovery to an Act of God.

And who is so cynical as to question the belief? Look around you, stranger, to contemplate the miracle of California as it appears today, after little more than a hundred years of statehood. Its north-south line extends 770 miles. Its coast line is 1200 miles long. It occupies the West Coast of the United States from Mexico to Oregon.

Californians have come almost automatically to think of it as two separate empires which they call Northern and Southern California. Now and then there is heated talk of demanding legislation to form two states. The dividing line would be along the Tehachapi Range.

It seems an unlikely step. California is, after all, the outstanding success story of all the West. In terms of population, the yardstick by which the West invariably gauges the importance of both its cities and its states, Los Angeles and California are beyond comparison anywhere between the Mississippi and the Pacific Coast.

But the matter does not stop with the Mississippi: California has already overhauled Pennsylvania, meanwhile winning eight new seats in Congress. The end is not yet. It seems probable that during the present decade California will displace New York as the most populous state.

One more statistic will wrap up both California and its largest city. I am indebted for it to Neil Morgan, columnist of the San Diego *Union,* who knows as much about the modern West as anybody. In order to give visitors an idea of the contrasts in population density of western states, Mr. Neil thoughtfully came up with this statement: "The casual student of maps which suggest only the vast dimensions of the West may like to know that of one hundred westerners in eleven states, fifty-eight are in California and twenty-five in metropolitan Los Angeles."

One may readily believe that to attract and hold ten and a half million persons, California must be favored by more than climate. Somewhere along the way were surely numbers of things which, when added together, comprise what realtors and others of ready imagination term "matchless opportunities." Yet Climate had been a factor from the first in turning casual visitors into permanent settlers. Even before the God-given millwright Jim Marshall had picked up the nuggets in the American River, and so loosed the Gold Rush of Forty-nine, the Yankee traders around Monterey, dealing largely in hides, had found the all but universal sunshine and blue sky to warrant favorable comparison with the Garden of Eden, along with other presumably mythical lands and climates of classic antiquity.

The first Easterners in this paradise came by ship, to find it a long settled civilization based on Spanish missions and Spanish ranches. It was charmingly mellow and indolent. Despite which, a revolt against Spain in Mexico City spread to what had been the Spanish province of California. Mexico declared its independence of Spain. California became a province of Mexico. By this time, numbers of Americans had infiltrated the region, among them the noted trapper and explorer, Jedediah Smith, who led the first overland party to reach the West Coast, and has been called the First Smith in California.

American settlers wanted California to join the United States, and soon arguments between American and Mexican settlers reached a dangerous stage. During 1844 American soldiers and navy ships were sent to California. The squabbles grew serious. Mexico demanded that the American commander, Captain John C. Frémont, remove his troops and ships out of California. Instead, he raised the American flag. The United States and Mexico went to war.

American settlers in California attacked and captured a Mexican fort, then unfurled a new flag. It bore a single star, a grizzly bear, and the legend CALIFORNIA REPUBLIC. Meanwhile United States troops in Mexico won the war. Mexico surrendered its claim to California Province, which soon became the thirty-first State of the Union.

Nine days before the treaty of peace was signed, James Marshall, soon to be the famous millwright, made his find. This is how it happened: Marshall had come down from Oregon in 1845, and gone to work building a sawmill near Sutter's Fort on the American River. His crew was a mixed lot—four Mormons, three Gentiles, and a number of Indians. They got the water wheel set too low. Marshall was a good millwright. He said the tailrace must be deepened. They would dig during the day, then let in the water at night to clean it out next day.

Next day was January 24, 1848, a Monday. On that morning Marshall turned the water out of the tailrace as usual, and along toward midafternoon he got down into it to see how much progress the water had made during the night. It wasn't much, for they were already down to bedrock. Only a few inches of water covered the granite shelf. Marshall saw something shiny under that water. He stooped to pick it up.

Within a few days, according to a favorite and possibly authentic account, Sam Brannan, a Mormon storekeeper at Sutter's Fort, ". . . bolted into San Francisco, and tore hatless through the old Plaza, crying out with his bull-throated bellow: 'Gold! Gold! Gold from the American River.' "

Before forty-eight was done, many thousands from the eastern United States had begun the staggering Rush of Forty-nine.

Although it was going to take an unconscionably long time to make the eastern United States comprehend the truly momentous event, the citizens of San Francisco were ready to believe Sam Brannan at once. Within a week after his wild announcement on the plaza, the city was being rapidly depopulated. Even crews of ships in the harbor deserted. All hands headed for John Sutter's mill on the American River.

By August of 1848 casual items about gold on the Pacific Coast were being run in eastern newspapers under small general headings such as "California Intelligence." Yet they had little or no effect. It was President James K. Polk's message to Congress in early December that touched off the mania—that plus a small chest of fine gold which was displayed in the War Office in Washington.

President Polk himself was anything but excited. "Recent discoveries render it probable," said he with the windy care of the politician, "that these mines are more extensive and valuable than was anticipated." It was doubtless the understatement of the decade. But it was, surely, official; and, too, there was that chest of yellow metal in the War Office. Delirium, said one observer, "seized upon the community of the District of Columbia."

Within a few weeks after Polk's guarded announcement, even the name of California was a symbol, an effulgent golden symbol, radiating the light that stemmed from Ophir on the darkest days—a promise of the metal that would unlock all doors, that would knit and break religions, that could crash the strongest barriers as easily as the lightning's bolt.

Credulity? It was as if everybody in the eastern United States was ready and anxious to believe that fine gold clustered around the root of every blade of grass that grew in California, that the streams there were clogged with it, that it bulged from the very hills and mountains. One of the first organized groups to get away was the Boston & California Joint Mining & Trading Company, 150 strong, whose 700-ton ship, the *Edward Everett,* sailed January 13 for San Francisco. In her hold were provisions and supplies sufficient to last two years. All contingencies were taken into consideration. On board were lightning rods and two brass cannon and a knockdown house complete, to be erected in San Francisco to serve as company headquarters. This was merely one of 275 vessels from American ports that docked there during 1849. Other ships had come or were coming from all over the world.

It seemed to many rushers that an unhealthy proportion of the immigrants had taken residence in San Francisco, and that far too many of them were assorted thugs. Vigilantes were organized in Sam Brannan's office, and he was elected their first president. They proceeded to take care of the worst of the city's criminals with dispatch, while Brannan gladly lent a hand to hang them.

The Rush rose and fell, then rose again as the Civil War was fought to a finish, and a new type of exodus to California began. It was soon stimulated and simplified by completion of the first continental railroad, which was the combined efforts of the Union Pacific and Central Pacific lines. The later arrivals were not prospectors, but homeseekers, and they did not concentrate on San Francisco, or even on the Mother Lode. They spread to every part of the state.

Among these thousands of new settlers one was Luther Calvin Tibbetts, born in Maine, whose influence on California was incomparable. Tibbetts deserves a statue or monument not only in the town of Riverside where he settled and worked his magic, but in every city, town, and hamlet in the vast orange-growing region. Tibbetts was the Seedless Orange Man.

Already middle-aged when he came West, Tibbetts was a great reader of government pamphlets having to do with agriculture, including soil analysis. He had found the fruit of the California orange trees was not particularly good, and it was filled with seeds. Now, if he could only reduce the number or eliminate the seeds . . .

After experimenting for several years on three small orange shoots sent him from Brazil in 1878, he was ready to show his fellow citizens what he had been up to. He invited them to his modest home to sample the new product. The oranges were sliced and passed around and lo! it was seen they contained not one seed. This in itself was most astonishing, probably as astonishing an event as southern California has witnessed. The seedless fruit was, moreover, of superb quality.

These Washington Navels, as Tibbetts called them, naturally could not be propagated by seed, but only by grafting. He was offered $10,000 each for his two surviving trees. He refused, and for the next several years sold buds from them. In 1880 a grove of seventy-five acres was set out to Tibbetts's Seedless by grafting buds to the stumps of the former trees. Within the year a syndicate planted an even greater tract, all from Tibbetts's buds. The mania for growing oranges was in full swing.

From here on, the story of Luther Tibbetts is a sad one. Litigation drained his new wealth. He lost home and property. His end came in 1902, in the county hospital at Riverside, a melancholy finish indeed for the man who had done so much to set off the boom by which Southern California caught up with and passed the northern section of the state. No other American appears to have contributed more to his adopted home. Yet the two Widney brothers from Ohio had much to do with turning the eyes of the world on Southern California.

Following his services as a post surgeon during the Apache wars in Arizona, Dr. Joseph P. Widney settled to practice in Los Angeles, where he organized the county medical society, served as the city's first health officer, and was elected president of the state board of health. In 1874 he and two other physicians issued a statement praising Los Angeles as a health resort, and invited settlement.

Meanwhile his brother, Robert M. Widney arrived in Los Angeles by stagecoach, a small trunk in his hand and a hundred dollars in his pocket, and lost no time in opening the city's first real estate office. Soon he was hauling prospects out over the rolling hills in a buckboard. "His optimism was complete," remarks Remi Nadeau, California historian who has specialized in his native Los Angeles where his own great-great-grandfather built the first four-story building.

"With Robert Widney," continues Nadeau, "Boosterism had arrived." In an early issue of his *Real Estate Advertiser,* Widney wrote that: "Heretofore underrated and misrepresented at home and abroad, Los Angeles county is rapidly assuming its proper place among the counties of the state." WATCH US GROW! was its cry, and its cry by repetition became hypnotic, fostering belief that Los Angeles was destined to be the greatest city in the greatest of all the states. When the boosters began their work, the only street paving was a layer of cast-off boots, dead animals, decayed vegetables and oranges, aromatic beyond description. Even at that early time rivalry had begun with the northern metropolis. "There are six murderers at present in the jail," bragged a Los Angeles newspaper. "There are only five in jail in San Francisco.

When California's only railroad, the Southern Pacific, was planning a second transcontinental line, Los Angeles voted a subsidy to the railroad on the promise that it should be on the main route. Two years later discovery was made that the road was trying to secure a right-of-way through Cajon Pass which could send trains whistling past a good thirty miles distant.

Having bought and paid for a main line, the Angelenos meant to keep it. "Led by Pioneer Booster Robert M. Widney," writes historian Nadeau, "surveyors for another local line were sent hurrying to Cajon Pass, and in the stategic narrows, where there was room for but one roadbed, they drove their stakes an hour before the S.P. men arrived. Meanwhile a telegram opposing the S.P.'s efforts was dispatched to Congress." The S.P. lost the pass.

A bit later the Southern Pacific's main line reached the city, and on its heels came the competing Santa Fe. And now the confident boosters launched the most persistent ballyhoo campaign the nation had ever seen. "Something about the California climate bred enthusiasm; eager to share their good fortune," so writes Angeleno Nadeau, "the Angelenos buttonholed the rest of the country and never let go."

Neither did the two competing railroads as they went headfirst into a stupendous knockdown rate war to carry the hordes to California. The Southern Pacific started things by putting on low-fare emigrant trains, composed of mere boxcars with cooking facilities. By early 1886, the cross-country fares, which had been at least $100 from Mississippi Valley points, were nosediving. Rates dropped so fast that passengers from the East were given rebates for price cuts made during the trip. The climax came on March 6, when the Santa Fe began the day with a $12 rate from Kansas City. The Southern Pacific countered with a $10 ticket. The Santa Fe dropped to $8; the Southern Pacific to $6, then to $4, and at last to $1.

One could hardly afford to stay at home. Although fares quickly rose, the rate from Kansas City did not exceed $25 for many months. And on came the multitudes, to be met with real estate prices that had risen considerably more than the cost of getting to California. Before the year was out, landowners were putting immense tracts, some of them already set out with Tibbett's new seedless oranges, up for auction sales of lots.

Brass bands met the prospective settlers, before whose eyes were unfurled gaudy banners to aid those of sluggish imaginations. All hands were offered a free ride and a free lunch. Few of the lemmings that fought for seats in the horse-drawn excursion buses had any idea of buying a lot, but the fast-working Angelenos knew better. "All you had to do was to get the prospect seated, and to keep talking . . ."

On they came by the thousands, and Los Angeles worked itself into a happy lunacy. "You could scarcely get anyone to talk about anything but real estate," is the way people remember it, but this is exaggeration; there were actually two topics: the price of a lot and the future of Los Angeles.

The Big Boom, however, included all of Southern California. One after the other, new towns took shape—Glendale, Burbank, Monrovia, Fullerton, Whittier, Inglewood. Hollywood began when Horace H. Wilcox opened a new subdivision which he planned to be a temperance colony. It grew steadily for a quarter of a century and was a respectable, churchgoing village of 4000 population before the first movie was made there. It is of record that this first Hollywood film was *The Law of the Range*, prophetic of the all-time favorite type of picture produced there for the past fifty years.

It mattered little if at all where a new subdivision was located. Were the townsite in the desert, it was advertised as a health resort; if a swamp, it was the site for a magnificent harbor; if on a mountain and barely accessible, why, mister, consider the glorious view! Dating from what turned out to be the top year of the current boom was the town of Azusa, a desolate stretch of sand and boulders. Of Azusa, its clear-eyed promoter said that, "If it wasn't good for a town, it isn't good for anything."

At the very height of the boom, writes historian Nadeau, "even the natives, who at first laughed up their sleeves at the prices they had wrung from the tenderfeet, were buying back at ten times the cost." By July of '87, lots were being sold like grain futures. Business was moving so deliriously that deeds could not be recorded fast enough. The crash was sudden. By April '88, everybody was trying desperately to get out from under.

Prices were slashed. Entire townsites went begging briefly, then reverted to the original owners. Paper towns disappeared as swiftly as they had come into being. The naked ribs of big hotels, crawling up the rolling hills of Los Angeles county, met quickie mansions, their Gothic windows broken, with now and then a cow gazing out through the sash.

The Big Boom had collapsed. Though the debris of dreams and fortunes was horrible to contemplate, when the dust cleared Los Angeles was seen to have become a metropolis of large brick buildings, paved streets, street lights, streetcars, complete with schools and churches. It had also dropped some 35,000 population within a couple of years.

Most important of all, observed historian Nadeau, the booster spirit—far from dying with the boom—"was fused into the Los Angeles mind, and, now broken to harness, it was put to work by the newly formed Chamber of Commerce. Bottled and corked, it was spoon-fed to every new arrival, whether he came by birth or rail. Los Angeles was going to be the biggest city in the world. The only question was how long would it take."

The Climate was still there, and so was the copperplated and double-distilled essence of Progress, Southern California brand. Even the Gods favored it. The wounds of the piteously battered region had not wholly healed when, in 1892, E. H. Doheny struck oil right in the middle of everything, and the stuff blew and ran until the lawns, chicken yards, and gardens were dotted with 1400 derricks, and the state of California was on its way to being the second-largest oil-producing state.

By 1920 the haughty San Franciscans could read, even in their own newspapers, that Los Angeles had passed their city in population and was still bragging it would overhaul Philadelphia, then Chicago. Long before drummers, salesmen, and even hobos had begun to speak of the new colossus as "L.A.," Los Angeles had become a favorite butt for all manner of jokes and gags. Its Men of Vision, the Boosters, were undergoing a continuous ribbing. Because of their ready acceptance of every fatuous reference to beauty, piety, learning, culture, or any other superior quality that could be associated with Southern California, they were easy marks for the hoots and cynical barbs of much of the rest of the state and, often, it must have seemed, of all other states.

It is to be doubted that any other city has grown and flourished on such a diet of ridicule and abuse as has been heaped on Los Angeles during the past sixty years. In truth, the city and its environs of claptrap communities earned the hostility. They got the swarming populations the Boosters wanted; and in those masses were appalling numbers of "leaders" who meant to lead the even larger numbers of faceless sheep bleating to be told what to do.

There is neither the wish nor the space here even to list the assorted mountebanks who rose and declined and disappeared during the decades. Early on the scene was a dedicated con man named Gaylord Wilshire whose very name is perpetuated by splendid Wilshire Boulevard which bisects Los Angeles and runs on and on until it plunges into the Pacific. Though he was defeated twice as a Socialist candidate for Congress, he was tolerant of capitalism; and made a modest fortune in billboard advertising before he bought a tract of sheep pasture at bargain rates and founded Fullerton, in the Los Angeles orbit, which, it is said, soon had the distinction of being "the richest city per capita in the world."

But Fullerton paled beside another achievement of Wilshire's; it was he whose *Wilshire's Magazine* converted Upton Sinclair to socialism. "It was like a falling down of prison walls about my mind," Sinclair recalled. "Wilshire's periodical was the most amazing discovery I ever made." Sinclair was perhaps the most voluble Socialist reformer in all California. He ran for Congress, for the Senate, and, after putting on false whiskers that fooled nobody, for governor. Whether or not he was politically envolved in a number of attempted reforms in California, it is mainly because of Sinclair that Southern Californians remember things called Technocracy, the Ham & Eggs movement, the EPIC aberration and, with a bow to Doc Townsend, the Old Age Revolving Pension Plan.

Sinclair found time also to urge adoption of Prohibition, Vegetarianism, and Telepathy, along with good words for Sylvester Graham, Ralph Bellamy, Josiah Warren, Ignatius Donnelly and, for all I know, spoke well for New Thought, Single Tax, and the Great I Am. It is recalled, too, that in the vast field of therapy Mr. Sinclair went whole-hog for Dr. Albert Abrams and his

Electronic Assembly, but ignored his good friend Wilshire's I-ON-A-Co, widely known as "Gaylord Wilshire's Magic Horse Collar."

Meanwhile, various Utopian settlements were tried, then petered out. Not even the depression years of the 1930s could stop the growth of the now fabled city. In fact, the incoming mobs grew in size and number. Up until the recent day when Los Angeles passed Philadelphia to become the third city, and seemed almost ready to pass Chicago, apparently no dedicated citizen of Los Angeles had thought of asking if population was an end in itself. More people, more customers, more business. Simple enough.

Yet there now came into the innermost secret reflections of the older residents a terrible thought, a question which the day before yesterday would have seemed downright wicked: Was it worth the cost to become the second-largest mass of population in the country?

Three-generation Angelo Remi Nadeau summed it up one day recently: Life in Southern California has become a huge jostling match. In San Fernando Valley, the city's last frontier, subdividers have built tract homes so hurriedly that schools, streets, sewers, fell years behind the need. Though haste had been made to complete construction of freeways, Los Angeles was now an immense traffic jam enveloped in smog. Often hidden from its own sunshine, the city was actually destroying its first resource —climate. Its long touted "wonderful soil" had been disappearing under a layer of pavement, roof tops, and swimming pools.

In closing his indictment, brave critic Nadeau remarks that: "Unable to stem the flood it started, Los Angeles was the victim of its own salesmanship. It was too late to wonder whether the Spanish might have been right after all. The only thing left was to build a city equal to the population."

It is of record that Dr. Joseph R. Widney, the famous old Booster who back in 1874 declared that as a health resort, Los Angeles stood alone, lived ninety-seven years and doubtless would have passed the century mark had he not suffered severe injury in an automobile accident. In any case, he had proved his assertion about healthful climate.

No such prophet seems to have arisen in California's second metropolis. The boosters of San Francisco had to get along as best they could with the delightful if often misty climate that marked the Golden Gate area of the Coast. But the location near the Mother Lode was responsible for the Rush of Forty-nine, and the Argonauts were not, after all, seeking health resorts.

Even a major earthquake in 1906 failed to shake faith in San Francisco, whose citizens have since tended to describe the almost total destruction of their town as due chiefly to "fire," as witness an often quoted quatrain dealing with the disaster:

> If, as they say, God spanked the town
> For being over-frisky,
> Why did He burn His Churches down
> And spare Hotaling's whiskey?

It seems that the warehouse stacked full of Hotaling's inflammables stood stanch and immune while scores of places of worship burned to the ground. A new San Francisco arose from the ruins, and it retained the position it had occupied since before the Gold Rush, when it started to crawl up the several steep hills from the original settlement called Yerba Buena. San Francisco is still the "capital" of the West Coast and the Far West. More than once it has been called "The New York City of the western United States."

As between behemoth Los Angeles and San Francisco's modest 775,000 citizens, there can no longer be said to be a "race" for population, if there ever was one. The backgrounds and attitudes of the two places are vastly different. By the time the first Los Angeles booster club was oiling its gears, San Francisco was long since famous the world over because of key position in relation to California gold. It was assured; possibly it was also a little superior in its dealings with what it termed the Real Estate Sharks of Southern California in general and specifically of Los Angeles.

Of more recent years, there has been a trend toward a sense of community feeling between Northern and Southern California. But it has not as yet, despite a good deal of arms-around-shoulders-singing "California Here I Come," dissipated the rivalry that called for Pistols for Two in older days.

If San Francisco robs New York City of its Major League Giants, Los Angeles steals the Dodgers from Brooklyn.

The University of California balances matters delicately by having a campus in the San Francisco area at Berkeley; and another, which is styled the University of California at Los Angeles. Could any Angeleno ask more in the way of identification?

During the years, both cities have been visited by labor troubles attended by violence so savage as to mark them as outstanding in the field of organized labor. On October 1, 1910, the Los Angeles *Times* building was wrecked by an explosion of dynamite. Twenty-one persons were killed.

In San Francisco, on July 22, 1916, ten lives were lost and many injured when a set-bomb blew up during a street parade.

That these two incidents were among the most spectacular of their kind in all the West, and that they both happened in California, the one in Los Angeles, the other in San Francisco, has prompted cynics to remark that even in the matter of publicity for its labor wars, California was bound it should be first and worst, at least anywhere west of Chicago.

Well, let it stand, if for no other reason than that of all western states, California is also the most volubly proud of its wonders, both natural and man-made. Perhaps one should rather include all forty-eight commonwealths, putting aside only Alaska

11. Even before the Gold Rush, the Yankee traders around Monterey had found the all but universal sunshine and blue sky to warrant favorable comparison to the Garden of Eden. (*Witch Tree, Monterey Peninsula*)

12. (*Mission Santa Barbara*)

13. Big Trees along the Generals Highway in Sequoia National Park.

14. The federal government has been generous in the matter of national parks and monuments, of which there are nine in California. (*Mount Whitney, Sequoia National Park*)

15. (*Half Dome from Sentinel Bridge, Yosemite National Park*)

16. Mount Shasta is in the Cascade Range of Northern California. It is an extinct volcano, with five glaciers on its slopes, a beautiful sight with its winter blanket of snow.

17. Donner Lake, 7000 feet high on Highway 40, has a monument in memory of the ill-fated Donner party which perished here in 1846.

18. If only for the sake of future poets, it is a pity that Utah was not permitted to enter the Union under its original name of Deseret. (*Cowboy Conference, Indian Creek, Utah*)

19. Waiting for the tourist in Utah are national parks and monuments of a number and quality beyond anything he has a right to expect of a single state. Zion National Park attracts nearly a million visitors annually; nearby Bryce Canyon (in photo above) fetches almost half a million.

20. The Yampa River canyon is a graveyard "where monstrous reptiles met a mysterious end." (*Split Mountain Gorge, Dinosaur National Monument, Utah*)

21. Said to be the largest natural bridge in the world, Rainbow Bridge was made a national monument in 1910 by President Taft. (*Rainbow Natural Bridge, Utah*)

22. Nevada is one of the larger states, and also one of the least populous, rating something like 1½ persons per square mile. (*Lake Tahoe, Nevada*)

23. (*Elephant Rock, Valley of Fire, Nevada*)

The Comstock Lode has been described as "a hundred miles to water, fifty miles to wood, a million miles to God, and three feet to Hell." The exaggeration is characteristic of the Nevada region.

24. Throughout the sixties and into the seventies, Virginia City (above) flowered as the swaggering metropolis of the Washoe. Its riches helped to finance the Union side of the Civil War.

and Hawaii on the ground they are still too new to warrant judgment as to their self-satisfaction.

Surely no other of the states has managed to turn its citizens into boosters of Minute Man quality, ready to ride and spread the alarm the moment anyone says, by word or in print, something inimical to the land of Gold and Climate. That this is so is by no means a coincidence. Almost from its admission, 153 years ago, California has instilled in its citizens a local patriotism that can be seen, heard and felt almost everywhere within its borders.

We outlanders should be glad that its chambers of commerce, its development commissions, its Friends of the Redwoods, of the Mother Lode, of thc Sierras, of Sutter's Mill, of the Vineyards, of the Camino Real; of the Sons and the Daughters of Native Sons, and the Granddaughters and Grandsons of same—that one and all these and other organized groups have long since documented every last Thing-to-See in the state.

These Things-to-See are not churlishly referred to as "Tourist Attractions" in California. Signs may direct and even urge you to see this or that along the way. So far as scenery is concerned, you are on your own, save possibly for an implication that you'd better look now at what is unique. And as for man-made marvels, including a large amount of roadside architecture, you will scarcely be able to avoid it. It will strike you between the eyes . . .

This is the right place to quote a poet, Keats, about the explorer, Hernando Cortes, who is believed to have discovered and named California:

Then felt I like some watcher of the skies
  When a new planet swims into his ken;
Or like stout Cortez when with eagle eyes
  He stared at the Pacific—and all his men
Look'd at each other with a wild surmise—
  Silent, upon a peak in Darien.

After living forty years in Oregon, which faces California on the north, I have naturally heard many people say what they most wanted to see in that state, and take it for granted that they did, indeed, visit the complex of towns and communities that constitutes Hollywood, the Film Capital of the World, the Home of Stars.

That this should be so is not a reflection on the state of culture in Oregon. I have reason to believe that the identical urge or preference would be voiced by a majority of tourists in Illinois, in Pennsylvania, New York, and even in Massachusetts. In other words, the Hollywood syndrome is a dominant subject in the minds of more Americans than I could wish were the case.

All I can say of Hollywood is that it is doubtless cognizant of its overpowering appeal as a Tourist Attraction, and hence is alert to the possibilities of public relations. And so, too, is the nearby metropolis of Los Angeles. "Glamorous" is a jim-dandy word in Southern California.

For other than those who come only for a load of unadulterated Hollywood, California offers as much to see as any state; and the good things are spread over the immense area of what is now exceeded by only Alaska and Texas. I've met tourists who professed, after a week's travel there, to have "covered California" from top to bottom of the map. These are braggarts. They have *not* seen California, nor even a minute part.

To begin with, the federal government has been generous in the matter of national parks and monuments, of which there are nine in California. If you approach from the Pacific Northwest, by way of Oregon, you will barely have passed the border when you come to the Lava Beds, a sort of never-never land of black labyrinth formed long ago when seventeen volcanic cones spewed rivers of fire and debris. In 1872 this area became a battleground when the Modocs left the reservation they had been unwillingly sharing with their ancient foes, the Klamaths, and, led by the able and notorious Captain Jack, took to the trenches and chasms of the Lava Beds and stood off army troops for many months.

In the same general area is Lassen Volcanic National Park where Lassen Peak, a supposedly long extinct volcano, suddenly roused to action in May 1914, and during three years belched lava, ash, and cinders, melted deep snow, and sent mud and boulders rolling into the valleys. Back in Gold Rush days, Mount Lassen was a 10,466-foot landmark to tell the hurrying migrants they were nearing the Sacramento diggings.

Swinging west to the Coast Highway and south almost to San Francisco, is Muir Woods, five hundred acres of virgin redwoods of the Coast variety, the Sequoia sempervirens. No camping here, yet this forest, named for the late naturalist John Muir, attracts half a million visitors annually. What brings many of them is partly its native quiet which ranges back a good 3000 years when these trees, not to be confused with the Sequoia gigantea of the Sierras, were springing as shoots from the ground cover. You'll find the Sequoia giants in both the Yosemite National and the Sequoia National parks in the California interior.

Trees loom large in the northern part of the state. In the south they may be said to loom curiously. Many a tourist never forgets his first sight of a Joshua tree, nor perhaps even his second, or hundredth look at the strange growth that is said to have been named by devout Mormons because its grotesque arms reminded them of Joshua at prayer. There are thousands of them in the national monument bearing their name where the Colorado and Mojave Deserts meet East of Los Angeles. Because this member of the lily family produces no telltale growth rings nobody knows how long it grows. Guesses as to the larger trees, forty feet tall, put the age at five hundred years.

There are still other national monuments and one more national park (Kings Canyon) scattered in California between Joshua Tree and the Lava Beds. These are Devils Postpile, Pinnacles, and Death Valley. The last named may or may not attract the most visitors, but is certainly the best known. Death Valley is a name to conjure with. Though the literati worked it over, to call a piece of it "Dante's View," this desert is still Death Valley and out of its hellish insides for twenty years on end came uncounted tons of borax, rolling behind the most spectacular freight service in North America, the twenty-mule-team wagons of the Harmony Borax Company. Another walking advertisement for Death Valley was Walter Scott, a character who carefully built himself into a legend under style of Death Valley Scotty, complete with $2 million castle, which is now a combination hotel and museum.

Of itself alone Death Valley was spectacular enough to warrant the distinction as a National Monument. Add those twenty-mule teams working a haul of 165 miles through the desert, plus a superb con man "desert rat" like Scotty, and Death Valley was unbeatable.

And this is as good a place as any to leave California for what, no matter where, simply has to be a state less favored by nature and, possibly, also less favored by the striking genius of its citizens, who now number, give or take, a few hundred thousand, no less than fifteen million.

In the West or, for that matter, in the United States one does not argue about a population of 15,000,000. California, to use an ultramodern term, has Got It Made.

UTAH MIGHT HAVE BEEN "DESERET"

Chapter Five

If only for the sake of future poets, it is a pity that Utah was not permitted to enter the Union under its original name of Deseret. "Deseret" has the sound of euphony, but what poet has been able to do much if anything with "Utah?"

In 1850, however, when Utah became a territory of the United States, there was little chance for "Deseret," even though it was the choice of its founders. It was a word from the Book of Mormon, meaning "honey bee." And by 1850, Mormons were as feared as they were disliked, and they had been harassed and already driven out of what most Americans believed and all Mormons hoped was United States territory.

Thus the school kids of early California described their state as bounded on the north by Oregon Territory, on the south by Mexico, on the west by the Pacific Ocean, and on the east by the territories of Utah and New Mexico. There were then no intervening Nevada and Arizona. For more than 600 miles Utah ranged across the Intermountain West into future Colorado.

Today's Utah ranks eleventh in area, and thirty-eighth in population, indicating a striking contrast between square miles and residents. The contrast seems even greater when you know that of Utah's present population of 890,000, more than one half live in the Salt Lake City area. Some 60 per cent of the population are members of the Church of Jesus Christ of Latter-day Saints. The visiting tourist, who cares to understand Utah, could hardly do better than to begin by contemplating the big orange lighted beehive that flashes atop the Mormon-owned Hotel Utah, in Salt Lake City, and another over its nearby motor lodge, on the other side of Temple Square.

The illuminated beehives, like Deseret, are potent symbols of the Latter-day Saints, or LDS, as they refer to themselves. Salt Lake City's evening paper is the *Deseret News.* The biggest department store in the state is Zion's Co-operative Mercantile Institution, Z.C.M.I. for short. The River Jordan empties into the Great Salt Lake. On every hand are reminders significant in Mormon history—Zion Savings and Loan; Deseret Roofing; Deseret Realty; Beehive Cafe; Beehive TV Repair; and Seagull Drugs. The last reference is to the swarms of birds that suddenly gathered, then flocked to destroy the cricket invasion that was ruining crops in 1848. The seagull is legally protected and held in reverence by all good Mormons.

The first thing the visitor will notice in Salt Lake City are the streets; they are 132 feet wide. The great Mormon leader, Brigham Young, is said to have prescribed this measure when the city was surveyed, more than a century ago. Traffic problems are still a minor municipal worry.

It is probable that in no part of the West will the visitor discover greater visible contrasts between the old and the new than in Utah. I don't mean just the conventionally "old" of pioneer days and conventionally "new" of automobiles and superhighways, but a very special sort of "old," of biblical reference that permeated the original Utah or Deseret territory, compared with the ultra "new" of the 1960s, when many Utahans are engaged in the manufacture of intercontinental ballistic missiles.

As Robert Cahn, an astute observer remarked recently in *The Saturday Evening Post,* "Utahns, who for years have had little to boast about except their educational system and spectacular scenery, look on with pride and amazement as their industrially delinquent state burgeons into one of the major arsenals of the West."

After a century of evolution from a religious empire to federal territory to statehood, the country of the Mormons finds itself in the midst of a still newer transition with the dawning of the space age. Alongside a rocket-engine test pad, the tourist will see cattle munching range grass. A reporter saw Navaho families living in mud-and-brush hogans. In a modern suburb of Salt Lake City, he talked with a grand-jury foreman who was "distressed with the practice of polygamy in his community." This remnant of early days is said to bc a rare holdover of a practice long since forbidden by the Church.

The use of "Gentile" to describe non-Mormons has pretty much faded away, but it survives to give point to what seems to be Utah's favorite Jewish story. It concerns the Jewish worker from an eastern state, who is quoted as saying of Utah: "I think this place is wonderful—such fresh air, such high mountains, and such friendly people. But I can't get used to being called a Gentile."

Like much of the West, Utah will eventually find itself overrun in season by tourists to whom the state presents not only more than its share of spectacular scenery, but to many visitors has the added appeal as the home country of the Mormons. And the Mormons turn out, even to the most hard-shelled of "Gentiles," to be as graciously hospitable as they are intelligent.

I recall more than a few tourists, not only from eastern states but from California, who have taken the pains to explain to me their astonishment that they had discovered "Mormons are just like other Americans." Although I may not have enthused overmuch with this "discovery" of alert tourists, I remained as tolerant as possible for a Gentile who was fairly familiar with the Book of Mormon, and has written about Mormons, both as people and as friends.

It is good that in this new era of tourism, visitors to Utah have been finding the state to contain its share of what they have come to see, in the esthetic matter of scenery, and also what just could be more than its expected share of hospitable people. Whether or not they have an interest in American history, they are also seeing a region second to no other western state in the drama of its background.

Western scenery is magnificent enough and to it has been devoted over many years an enormous literature that mounts steadily from the hurried and breathless pamphlets of the professional boosters to some really excellent verse by our poets. I'd rather not attempt to add to this literature, even though I probably enjoy a dramatic or a soothing scene as well as the next man. But often I enjoy it more if I know it was once witness to some piece of history—say the Custer Battleground in Montana; the site of Lewis and Clark's camp in Oregon; and where the Rails Met and the Golden Spike Was Set at Promontory Point, sixty miles West of Ogden, Utah.

For example, from where I write I can see the immensity of Mount Hood in Oregon. There it stands, alone, aloof, complete, majestic. It is a superb sight. Yet I never look upon it without thinking of the Crag Rats of Hood River, near its base, who again and again over the years have crawled over the mountain's inhospitable flanks, braved its blizzards and its crevices, and otherwise risked and even lost their lives to rescue somebody described as a sports enthusiast, who obviously should have never been permitted to go above timber line on Mount Hood.

For the same reason, which has to do only with the imagination, I should as soon stand by the stark monument in Salt Lake City that marks the spot where Brigham Young said, "This is the place," as view all the natural wonders of Zion National Park, *and* Bryce Canyon.

Imagination peoples the Mormon story from the Hill Cumorah in upper New York State to the founding of Deseret in Utah in 1847, then onto the tardy admission to the Union in 1896.

The history of Utah is unique. Its pioneers were not like any other pioneers anywhere. They were Mormons, members of a native American sect founded in 1831 by Joseph Smith, Jr., a Vermonter who had migrated to New York. Persecution caused the Church of Jesus Christ of Latter-day Saints to grow amazingly. Both persecution and growth continued as the Saints moved again, into Illinois and Missouri. In Illinois prophet Smith founded a city, Nauvoo. Within five years it was the largest town in the state, and Smith announced his candidacy for the presidency of the United States.

Troubles were brewing between the Mormons and all others, called Gentiles by the Saints. In June 1844, prophet Smith was shot and killed by a mob who stormed the jail where the Mormon leader was held on a pledge of protection. Brigham Young was accorded leadership of the Church.

Here, surely, was one of the greatest natural leaders produced in the United States, a major figure in western history. With enormous energy and great vision, Brigham Young made plans to remove the Saints beyond the jurisdiction of the United States. He sent forth his most trusted men to scout the country. While working slowly westward, these advance groups built bridges and houses and put in crops for others who would follow. They also mustered a Mormon Battalion of five hundred soldiers for service in the war against Mexico. This battalion left Iowa to walk some two thousand miles to California.

Then, in January 1847, Brigham Young announced that the general place of settlement had been determined; it was to be somewhere in the valley of the Great Salt Lake. Only the specific spot remained to be chosen. On moved the Mormon pioneers, up the North Platte, then along the Oregon Trail, to confer with Jim Bridger and other mountain men, and to push on from Fort Bridger into Salt Lake Valley. During July 21–24, the Mormon pioneers entered the valley, and plowing began. Young, who had been ill with mountain fever, arrived on the historic twenty-fourth. Ill or not, he was the sort of man who knew where he was. "This is the place," he said simply. And it *was*, the capital of the Saints, where they lost no time in breaking the soil. Here in the desert they should make the rose to bloom.

Above all, Brigham Young wanted his people to settle in a spot as isolated as possible from Gentiles. By an irony of fate, the Salt Lake Valley was virtually athwart what in 1847 was the well-defined Oregon Trail and in less than two years more was also the trail to California which was to say, the Gold Diggings, the route of the Forty-niners.

Though Young was determined that Mormons were not to go seeking minerals, they were exposed to the corruptive thousands of wild men who paused on their way West, and bought supplies at famine prices from the Saints. No other settlers of the time were subject to such discipline as drove the Mormons to incredible efforts—irrigation canals quickly brought the desert to heel; plowed and fenced farms marked the valleys; so did settlements. That the Church was ever present could be seen by the very names of the villages—Lehi, Moab, Deseret, Ephraim, Manti. These and others came from The Book, and the Book of Mormon was interpreted as need arose from time to time by leader Young, and explained to the faithful by lay bishops in charge of the wards, the divisions of the Church, each ward containing from five hundred to a thousand members.

Work? There can be little doubt that Mormons worked harder, longer and to better purpose than did most Gentile settlers. It was a tenet of the Church, too, that strength lay in unity and co-operation. This was, and to a large extent still is, where the Mormons shine. The Church was a stern master. It had no time for softies. Alcohol, tobacco, coffee, and tea were forbidden.

It is not to be thought that so self-reliant a minority was to be permitted to prosper in isolation. In 1856, a time when the United States was about ready to split over the issue of slavery, the two major political parties, possibly to divert public attention from the real subject, bethought themselves of the *twin* "relics of barbarism," one of which was polygamy, otherwise described "as the loathsome ulcer on the body politic."

Only a bit later it was alleged in Congress that the Mormons were in open rebellion. President Buchanan directed General W. S. Harney to proceed to Utah Territory and put down the rebellion. Governor Brigham Young declared martial law in the Territory. To the Mormon colonies in Nevada and California he sent orders to gather in Zion. The Utah militia and the Nauvoo Legion began drilling. Mormon Commander Lot Smith was dispatched to harass the government wagon trains on the way to rebellious Utah. He struck quickly and hard. He first burned all available forage between South Pass and Fort Bridger; then cut off the advance army supply trains and put them to the torch. Then, swinging in behind the main column of the Army's Utah Expedition, he destroyed it.

The federals went into winter quarters near Fort Bridger, some three hundred miles short of their objective.

What became known as the Mormon War, or the Utah War, occupied federal troops and Mormons until the outbreak of the War between the States in 1861. When the greater struggle began, Heber C. Kimball, Brigham Young's first counselor, was ready to state the Mormon's position. "We shall never secede from the Constitution," he declared. "We shall not stop on the way of progress, but we shall make preparations for future events. The South will secede from the North, and the North will secede from us, and God will make the people free as fast as we are able to bear it."

The Saints promptly drew up their third constitution for a "State of Deseret," elected Brigham Young governor, and a legislature, then dispatched to Congress a memorial seeking admission to the Union. Congress, instead, passed a new law aimed at the practice of polygamy, and sent a regiment of volunteers into Utah to pitch their camp on a bend above Salt Lake City and unlimber their artillery within range of Brigham Young's residence.

Despite the failure of Congress to recognize the Mormon petition, the members of the Deseret legislature met this and every succeeding year until 1870, a total of nine sessions. Meanwhile, the first transcontinental railroad passed through Utah, and its two sections were joined with the classic Golden Spike ceremonies near Ogden.

Long before the railroad, but only after many years of agitation, the people in western Utah, mostly Gentiles, succeeded in persuading Congress to organize in 1861 the Territory of Nevada, and all of Utah west of 116° west longitude was lost to the new Territory. At the same time, Colorado Territory was formed by cutting off all the country between the summits of the Rockies and 109° west of Greenwich. A final slice of Utah was taken in 1868, to complete the rectangle created as Wyoming.

Statehood was not given to Utah until 1896 when, on January 4, President Grover Cleveland proclaimed it the forty-fifth state of the Union. Polygamy had been officially abandoned by the Church in 1890.

One of the first acts of the brand new state of Utah was to grant women the vote, the third state to do so. It was signed by Utah's first governor, Heber M. Wells, whose wife Emmaline had long been a stanch worker for female suffrage. The second act passed by the new legislature had to deal with a delicate situation brought about by the Enabling Act that created the state of Utah. The new problem was this: Whether those who had already contracted a polygamous marriage should be permitted to continue living in polygamy, or whether polygamous living itself should be prohibited. The more humane alternative was adopted.

The scars left by some forty years of contention and violence healed slowly. Mormon and Gentile worked together, most reluctantly at first. Water shortage prevented expansion of agriculture. Because of high freight rates, manufacturing was slow to develop. The load on taxpayers increased as vast tracts of land were withdrawn from the tax rolls. (Almost 80 per cent of present Utah is now in federal or state hands. Example: One military proving ground occupies an area larger than Rhode

Island.) There was also the Mormon tradition of large families and the demand that children be competently schooled.

With the railroads, especially as the gigantic mineral wealth of Utah became apparent, came the steady arrival of non-Mormon settlers looking for opportunities which, ever since the first, had habitually if doctrinately been ignored by the Saints. Minerals have long since become the largest single natural resource. What is known as the Kennecott Copper interests has the state's biggest payroll. Hercules Powder has been making explosives for use in mining and construction since World War I. Today Hercules is also in the guided missile business, and in the plant are 1000 missile workers, and only 90 making dynamite. A division of Sperry Rand, with 3000 employees, is one of the biggest missile makers in the Salt Lake Region.

Utah's second city, Ogden, was originally the town that "got the railroad," that made good when the Union Pacific made it the rail center of the intermountain West. Around or near it today is a complex of industries and the Hill Air Force Base, with some 12,000 civilians on the payroll. Another 1000 workers will converge there before long when Boeing Airplane opens a plant to assemble Minuteman missiles, or whatever by then happens to be the latest thing in America's arsenal.

Let the visitor rest assured, however, that Utah's new role in what is called the Space Age has as yet had no effect on the natural wonders on view in Utah. The tourist with less than many weeks on his hands will be hard put to know where to begin. Waiting for him are national parks and monuments of a number and quality beyond anything he has a right to expect of a single state.

Zion National Park attracts nearly a million visitors annually. Nearby Bryce Canyon fetches almost half a million. There are five other distinct reservations listed as Monuments which, if added to the intinerary, would fill the average tourist's summer vacation to its last day and show no strain, though the tourist himself would.

Only thirty-five miles from Salt Lake City is Timpanogos Cave in the Wasatch Mountains. If it's rock arches you want, go on to Moab and Arches National Monument, long ago described by cowboys as, "Nothing out there to see, jest a lot of holes in rocks." These ribbons of stone are less well known than Utah's natural bridges, but they have many devotees who consider that one delicate arch, 85 feet high and 65 feet wide, has no competition as the most weirdly beautiful object in all outdoors.

There are two monuments devoted to natural bridges in Utah. One has to do with several bridges, the other, near the Arizona border, is dedicated to Rainbow Bridge. Said to be the largest natural bridge in the world, it was made a national monument in 1910 by President Taft.

Straddling the Colorado border in northeast Utah is Dinosaur National Monument. The pitch here is that the Yampa River canyon is a graveyard "where monstrous reptiles met a mysterious end." The names of two other monuments, Cedar Breaks and Capitol Reef, do not indicate why they are reservations. The first was named by Mormon settlers who called junipers cedars; and "breaks" are cliffs near a mesa's edge. The scene is a huge amphitheater, cut from pink cliffs, with ridges radiating toward the cliff arc like painted spokes of a circus-wagon wheel.

In pioneer times Capitol Reef, called the Waterpocket Fold, brought westbound wagons to a halt. In 150 miles it could be crossed only in three places. The Reef is still rated by natives as "rugged country."

If visitors do not feel like facing long drives and rugged country, they need not leave the Salt Lake region at all. Within that city's orbit are a number of unusual things worth seeing to keep one occupied for several days. For instance, the complex of ghost mining towns in the Oquirrh Mountains, others in the Wasatch Mountains, and a few more in the East Tintic region a little southwest of Utah Lake. All are within a radius of fifty miles or so from the capital city.

From the steps of the state capitol building one can just make out the white terraces of the tremendous open-pit mine of Kennecott Copper at Bingham Canyon. For several reasons, and not because it is the biggest mine of its kind in the United States, Bingham Canyon is something not to be missed—that is, not by the many tourists who find western ghost towns most appealing to the imagination. Hundreds of exhausted mines in the West manage to support a store, a saloon, curio shops, and a service station merely because of their flavor of the past.

Bingham Canyon is not ghostly. Since 1863 mines here have been shipping ore rich in silver, gold, lead, and copper; and some two billion dollars' in copper alone have come from the canyon since Daniel C. Jackling changed the style of mining from deep-hole to open-pit. There are said to be sufficient ore bodies left to keep the present Kennecott Copper Corporation going for another quarter of a century. Yet the place has the special flavor of the past and no mining-town fan will be disappointed in the one narrow street that crowds the canyon for more than seven miles.

The sheer sides of the canyon are terraced benches, rising tier upon tier until they disappear from sight. The houses press hard against the walls, lest they encroach on the pavement. Crammed tight between the houses are power stations, mine buildings, schoolhouses and concrete playgrounds enclosed by wire-mesh fences. Some of the houses are freshly painted, but mostly they are weathered and dingy and monotonously gray. That observant specialist in western ghost towns, Muriel Sibell Wolle, found Bingham Canyon both eerie and dramatic. Others have found it to be as ugly as sin. None seem to have been indifferent to the mine itself.

You come to this open pit after passing through a tunnel to face something awesome. If the Pyramids are great, then so is this vast hole at Bingham Canyon, with its twenty-odd levels and ninety miles of railroad track, along which the long ore trains are moving from level to level, from top to the bottom of this 2000-foot-deep pit. Out of this hole, since the first steam shovel began its gouging, has come enough rock to bury Salt Lake City to a depth of fifteen feet, and enough copper to put a band two feet wide around the globe.

From Bingham, the dedicated inspector of ghost towns can, by relatively short drives reach many more. They will be found in various stages of obsolescence, and even ruin, and the would-be visitor will do well to make inquiry, before he strikes out to see Stockton, Ophir, Mercur, Silver City, Mammoth, Eureka, and Park City.

Local critics of Salt Lake City like to point out that during the past thirty-three years only one major building has been added to its skyline. They complain that the city has grown sparingly since the state's new prosperity came to its suburban areas through their involvement in manufacturing for what so glibly is called the Space Age. These strictures leave at least a few of us unmoved about the plight of a town which has failed to keep in stride with fortunate Los Angeles, which has already achieved a population of three million plus an atmospheric density of smog.

It has taken more than a century for Salt Lake City to gain a population of less than 200,000, while Utah, eleventh in rank in area, ranks thirty-eighth in population. This ratio of people to square miles is as healthy a condition as a rational man could wish. It indicates that the booster types are far from dominating either Salt Lake City or Utah. If this is not unique in all the West, then somebody has been fudging with the statistics of PROGRESS.

But Utah and Salt Lake City *are* unique. Twenty years of discipline, and environment, plus the leadership of Brigham Young, one of the very great leaders the world has known, had made of the Mormons the perfect pioneers of the American West. Continuous persecution served merely to convince them in their belief that they were, indeed, the Chosen People of the Lord to make the desert blossom as the rose.

Though the non-Mormon visitor to Salt Lake City is not likely to be urged to visit Mormon institutions there, and is even forbid to enter the Temple, the intellectually curious will find a day or two in the city most rewarding. He may begin almost anywhere in the Temple Square area, the heart of the Mormon world, in downtown Salt Lake City.

The Temple itself is used exclusively by members of the Church for baptismals for the living and the dead, for "sealing" ceremonies, and marriages. Ground was broken in 1853, but work was suspended in 1857 just before federal troops arrived to put down the "Mormon Rebellion," and resumed later. The walls were twenty feet high when Brigham Young died in 1877, and construction was not finished until 1893, forty years to a day after it was begun. Above its highest tower is the gilded copper image of the angel Moroni, the revelator of the Mormon doctrine.

The Tabernacle is used for the spring and fall conferences of the Church, and often for civic events. The auditorium seats 5000 and its acoustics are such that, when it is vacant, a pin dropped can be heard more than 200 feet distant. The Tabernacle organ, and its 300-voice choir, is known the country over for its Sunday broadcasts. Free organ recitals are given weekdays, with the public invited.

Perhaps the structure of greatest curiosity to Gentiles is the Lion House. The name comes from the carved stone lion, done by a pioneer craftsman, which stands over the first-floor portico, and the house is now used as a social center and banquet hall by Mormon Church organizations. But it wasn't always thus, for once upon a time it housed several of Brigham Young's wives, and it still presents no fewer than twenty steep-roofed gables. Hence thc interest of strangers in the city. Did ten wives live here, or twenty?

Brigham Young did nothing to clear this matter. It is said he took delight in confusing the guessers. The occupants were of no help: "The face of a woman is rarely seen at a window, and her voice is never heard from without."

Adjacent to the Lion House is the church historian's office and library. Because a tenet of the Church prescribes that every Mormon prepare as far as possible a genealogical record of his or her family, no LDS officer is of more importance than the historian. Visitors from afar come here to fill vacant spots in family records, and those who cannot come in person do what they can by mail.

The Beehive House, dating from 1855, was built for the residence of Brigham Young, a gracious mansion much like those characteristic of Salem and Newburyport, Massachusetts, even to a widow's walk on the roof, 3000 miles from the Atlantic Ocean. The Mormon symbol is enclosed in a cupola. The interior of this astonishing house is worthy of study to reveal the ingenuity of the early carvers, who "varied their patterns up with the stairs, moved out to greet the landings, then swept on to higher levels."

In Temple Square are two markers of especial significance to Mormons. One is the Three Witnesses Monument, a block of granite with bronze bas-relief likenesses of Oliver Cowdery, David Whitner, and Martin Harris, who testified that an apparition showed them the golden plates from which the Book of Mormon was translated. (The monument is the work of Avard Fairbanks.) The other memorial comprises the statues of Joseph and Hyrum Smith, life-size bronzes of the Mormon prophet and his brother, martyred in Carthage, Illinois, in 1844. Both works were executed by Mahroni Young, a grandson of the Mormon leader.

Then there is the Museum of the Latter-day Saints. The tourist had best begin here, or leave it for the last, for in it is a collection of objects of such variety they add up to a visual grass-roots history of the Church. Visitors are commonly assigned to Mormon guides, who are as courteous as they are easily informative. They can explain the relics of the famous handcart migration from Missouri to Salt Lake City when some 4000 persons crossed the plains by this primitive method. There was nothing else like it in the history of the American West.

But it would be futile to try even to list the things on display in this "treasure house" of Mormon history. If the tourist can visit, say, but one of the many "attractions" in Salt Lake City, then let it be the museum. He will go away with some idea of dedicated spirit that went into the building of the State of Deseret which was to become Utah, whose state flag shows a beehive, and the word INDUSTRY.

NEVADA

Chapter Six

The irony that removed Nevada from what for a decade had been Utah Territory has been unmatched in the history of the American West. The Mormons remained in charge of their religious province. New Nevada went into the business as proprietor of the Comstock Lode, which has been described as "a hundred miles to water, fifty miles to wood, a million miles to God, and three feet to Hell."

The exaggeration is characteristic of the region in that it contains enough substance to typify the contrast between Utah and Nevada to the present day. In Utah is an attitude of more than average influence in support of conventional morals. In Nevada the attitude is one of infinite toleration. There is no need here to go deeper into what are conventional morals, which have nothing to do with the rare beauty of these desert states, or of people who live there.

On the mental maps of most Americans, Nevada is one of those "white space" regions designated in older geographies and marked with legends of GREAT DESERT and SAGE PLAINS and SAND HILLOCKS. It is one of the larger states, and also one of the least populous, rating something like 1½ persons per square mile. I like the way a cartographer saw it for Rand McNally Frontier Atlas of the American West:

> Somberly magnificent and infinitely moody, Nevada is a high, arid land lying mostly in the Great Basin, with a few serrated valleys sloping off toward the unfriendly Colorado River. Mountains march across this land; they rise as tall peaks, shining with snow or hazed with blue; they lift ocherous ridges stained angry purple and fiery black by some age-old agony of the earth. Valleys awesome in their emptiness roll away under dark junipers and velvety sage . . .

Into and across this empty land passed the Forty-niners on the way to the California gold fields; and a decade later they and thousands more returned to Nevada in tidal waves to dig in ledges of silver that went into history as the Comstock Lode. For nearly a century one mining boom after another of silver or gold kept generations of Nevadans stirred up and on the move, first into one, then another, portion of their vast desert. Much silver, a lot of copper, and no little gold and other metals have come out of Nevada ground.

For fully as long, wildcat promotion helped to create an atmosphere calculated to instill and maintain a continuous gambling fever. In those times every town had its faro bank, along with a perpetual poker game and monte dealers beyond count. Gaming was associated with saloons, and for decades the characteristic combination was a large room down one side of which ran the bar, while ranged along the opposite wall were the faro bank, the wheels, and the dice and card games.

Then, in 1879, a law provided for the state licensing of gaming houses. This was a revenue raising measure, both lax and mild, and seems to have had little effect one way or another. But in 1909 something happened to the legislature. It passed an act abolishing all games of chance. For the first time Nevadans were prohibited from patronizing what for sixty years had been their chief form of entertainment. The act was, of course, a mistake and a failure. It merely drove gambling underground—

though not very far. Modifications of the act were made in 1912, again in 1913, and finally it was repealed in 1931. A new law went on the books. It permitted, as it does today, virtually everything in the way of gambling, save lotteries. It provides for license fees, and it also taxes the gross take, the "handle" as it is known.

This is the place to pause in the narrative, to say something of Nevada in its roaring great days of the Comstock Lode, and to trace the steps by which the state became the one single spot in continental United States where all kinds of gambling are not only legal but are Nevada's largest industry, beside which mining is less than peanuts.

The rush to the Comstock got its start in Grass Valley, one of California's fading gold camps in the summer of 1859, when a weary traveler hove in with some chunks of gold-bearing ore which he said he picked up in the Washoe country of western Utah Territory. Next day, Grass Valley's leading assayer tested the rock and was bug-eyed to find it ran to about $1000 to the ton in gold, plus a much higher content of silver. "At least $3500 a ton," he said.

Within hours, the town of Grass Valley had begun to boil over. Judge James Walsh, old mining hand and a friend of the stranger from Washoe, piled provisions on a mule and struck out ahorseback for Nevada City and the trail over the Sierra to the Washoe region of western Utah Territory. With him was George Hearst, a young mining man, and Atwood, the assayer. Almost on their heels was a crew of other fast movers. They all converged on Sun Mountain to find the two discoverers, Peter O'Riley and Pat McLaughlin, at work. One of these sold his share for $3000 to Hearst. Judge Walsh paid $11,000 for the alleged interest of Henry Comstock, who had talked himself into a one-third share with the two discoverers.

By late summer, Walsh and Hearst were shipping ore over the Sierra by muleback 160 miles, and another 80 miles by steamer. It was so heavy in gold and silver that it could be smelted in San Francisco at a spectacular profit. By winter California papers were quoting Comstock assay figures. Before spring, bars of pure Washoe silver were being displayed in the windows of banks. And an army of prospectors was watching the melting snow in the passes.

Soon the adventurers were pushing up through the Sierra pines, forming an unbroken line of men, mules, and wagons from the Sacramento Valley to the Carson Valley. In a little, too, there came seekers from the East. Disappointed by the gold rush to Pikes Peak, they had moved on, thinking to try California, but had been stopped by the stampede to Washoe.

By another spring, the Comstock mania was reaching its peak. Extensions of the lode indicated a width and depth and richness almost unbelievable. An observer at a new camp named Virginia City estimated that "only one inhabitant in fifty is actually mining the earth." A few more were out prospecting for new leads, but by far the greatest number was engaged in buying and selling shares. He complained that his twenty roommates in a Virginia City hotel spent most of the night trading claims and showing each other samples of ore. Newspapers in San Francisco and New York City were already listing shares and prices of Comstock mines, real and alleged, by the columnful.

Throughout the sixties and into the seventies, the wealth of the Comstock was the first fact of economics on the Pacific Coast. Virginia City flowered as the swaggering metropolis of the Washoe. Its riches helped to finance the Union side of the Civil War. Its International Hotel was the most luxurious between Chicago and San Francisco. Its Virginia & Truckee Railroad met the transcontinentals at Reno, and operated sleepers, diners, and parlor cars between Virginia City and San Francisco. It carried the newly made Comstock millionaires, and their friends who came to visit the mines; and also the innumerable theatrical stars bound for Piper's Opera House. Its leading daily, the *Territorial Enterprise*, had on its staff reporter Samuel Clemens, better known as Mark Twain. Its mining editor was famous as Dan DeQuille.

Virginia City was the most important outpost of Wells, Fargo & Company, the powerful banking and express firm. Millionaires associated with Virginia City and its mines included James Flood, Jim Fair, Adolph Sutro, George Hearst, and William Sharon. Richest of all was John Mackay. Of these nabobs, historian Lucius Beebe has written that: "Little of the great wealth produced by the Comstock remained in Nevada, in contrast with Colorado, where the great fortunes made by the mines of Leadville, Central City, and Cripple Creek found their way to Denver and Colorado Springs where they remain to the present time."

"With the sole exception of John Mackay," writes Beebe, "the nabobs of Virginia City looted and left. Their monuments are mostly in San Francisco, where the Palace Hotel, the Hearst newspaper, the Fairmont hotel, the Flood and Sharon buildings, Roos Brothers department store, the Wells Fargo Bank & Union Trust Company, all bear witness to the wealth removed from the deep mines of the Comstock.

"Little stayed in Nevada save Mackay's endowments of a Catholic Church in Virginia City, and the Mackay School of Mines, which is a part of the University at Reno."

When the Comstock reached its zenith, and production began slowly to fall off, the prospectors and the speculators began looking for new bonanzas. Several strikes were made elsewhere in Nevada, such as Austin, Hamilton, and Ely in the eastern part of the state. The various camps rose, prospered, then faded. Between 1878 and 1900, for instance, mining income in the state dropped from $47 million to less than $3 million.

During this long period, however, so conditioned to speculation had Nevadans become, that trading in mine stocks continued comparatively active. But actual mining was virtually at a standstill. That is, until the late summer of 1900, when Big Jim Butler, a rancher in central Nevada near Belmont, who had a lot of time on his hands, which he spent in what he admitted was his favorite if useless pastime of prospecting, chipped a ledge which local Indians called "Tonopah," allegedly meaning "hidden spring water." He put the sample in his pocket.

Butler was no man in a hurry. He made several futile efforts to have his sample assayed on one of those standard promise deals—"I'll cut you in on it." But Butler tried again, this time leaving the sample with Tasker L. Oddie, a young lawyer from New York who had come West to look after some mining property for Anson Phelps Stokes. Oddie had an assay made. The specimen tested out at $600 a ton in gold and silver, mostly gold.

While this event was taking place, Butler and his wife were busy haying on their ranch forty-five miles away, and when an Indian runner brought the news from Oddie, the Butlers refused to get excited. Not until almost three months later, when the hay crop was in, did Butler and his wife set out in a most leisurely manner for Tonopah.

It was August 25, 1900, when the Butlers located the Desert Queen for themselves and an adjoining claim, the Burro, for Oddie. When Mrs. Butler noticed a likely outcropping, she located what turned out to be the most valuable claim of all, the Mizpah.

Before the Butlers left the scene of discovery, they went on to locate the Valley View, Silver Top, and Buckboard claims which, so mine historian Glenn Quiett wrote, were combined to form the famous Tonopah property, estimated to have added $150 million in gold and silver to Nevada's production. By the time Tonopah grew into a sizable camp, complete with saloons, brothels, gambling clubs, and stores, a professional gambler, George Wingfield, had struck gold not far from the growing new camp. This was to be Goldfield, and almost overnight Goldfield brought a stampede.

Was this new bonanza region to be the Comstock all over again? The Southern Pacific railroad started building a branch line. It reached Tonopah in 1904, and Goldfield in 1905. Other towns were being born of strikes south of Goldfield, and named Bullfrog and Rhyolite and Rawhide. One gets an idea of the size of this last major stampede in Nevada by knowing that when the railroad reached Goldfield, that town had 15,000 people, five banks, five hotels, a Turkish bath, a florist, two hospitals, and a restaurant, the Palms, decorated at a cost of $12,000. It boasted a string orchestra. In Goldfield, too, was the Northern Saloon, Tex Rickard, Prop., which employed twenty-four bartenders, and eighty-five housemen to tend the games.

Rickard was a really great promoter. In 1906, he staged in Goldfield a prize fight between Battling Nelson and Joe Gans for the lightweight championship of the world. It was the first of Rickard's so-called Battles of the Century. It brought an immense crowd. The gate passed $78,000. Under the hot desert sun, the fight went on for forty-two rounds. The climax came when a low blow sent Gans to the canvas writhing with pain, and the referee awarded the contest to Gans. Battling Nelson's manager threatened suit, but thought better of it.

The fight put Goldfield on the map from Tampa to Tacoma. More importantly, it made the task of wildcat promoters of Nevada mining stocks easier even than before. Right after the fight, speculation leaped high. In 1907, the Goldfield Mining Exchange had to close for several days to catch up with orders. And in New York, stocks were sold from third-floor windows of the Curb Exchange to crowds in the streets. A billion dollars in doubtful shares were issued, and $100 million of it was sold in Nevada, from the five hundred issues listed on the Goldfield Exchange.

For another brief hour, Goldfield reveled in the wild boom unmatched in intensity by anything that had gone before, in Nevada or elsewhere. Population of the town passed 22,000. Strikes shook the town, and the Wobblies (Industrial Workers of the World) moved in to stage riots, but actual mining continued, and speculation rose to new heights. Time, however, was working. Within five years Goldfield's population dropped from its top figure to 3500 in 1914. And by 1919, the Goldfield Consolidated closed its stamp mills, having paid $30 million in dividends.

In 1923, a fire destroyed most of the fading town, including fifty-two solid blocks of the business district. Two cloudbursts in 1931 completed the job, leaving Goldfield with a few hundred people, and its million-dollar hotel to stand in dreary grandeur. The other camps in the district went much the same way. Of them all, Rhyolite perhaps went the quickest. The end was so sudden that the railroad carried thousands of penniless miners out of the country free of charge. Rhyolite, with the remains of large modern brick and stone business blocks still standing, became the desert's most spectacular ghost town.

By the time Rhyolite and most of the older mining towns in Nevada had faded, the state found itself with nearly empty coffers. After all, it had relied from the first on mining. During the generally booming 1920s, Nevada had managed to get along only because of its liberal divorce laws, its continued tolerance of gambling, and a notable lax enforcement of the Volstead Act. If the state came to be looked upon as a maverick, a sort of obstreperous problem child in the family of states, as Oscar Lewis has pointed out,[1] this "did not greatly disturb the generality of the natives."

As time passed, Nevadans could no longer be blind to the abuses that had grown up in their free and easy system. Why not legalize gambling and thus bring it out into the open where it could be controlled? When the legislature met in 1931, there was a demand by citizens, led by Governor Fred Balzar, himself of pioneer Nevada stock, to repeal the ineffectual laws about gambling, and to make gambling as much an industry as mining or ranching. After three weeks of heated debate, a new and sweeping act was passed.

The legislation provided for the immediate lifting of the ban on gambling all over the state, and the state responded by staging a celebration that lasted a full week. The public response was immediate. Throngs crowded the gaming rooms in Reno and lesser towns, the owners of which were already preparing to move out of their obscure hideaways into ground-floor quar-

[1] *Sagebrush Casinos, The Story of Legal Gambling in Nevada,* 1953.

ters on the busiest streets. In California, word got around quickly that on the other side of the state line gambling was both legal and wide open, and "thousands hurried to try their luck under these novel conditions, thus becoming the forerunners of concerted weekend migrations across the Sierra that have continued ever since."

Yet, for six years after repeal, gaming-house operators did nothing to publicize their establishments. "They could not," Mr. Lewis writes, "bring themselves to court the public attention they had so long been at some pains to avoid." In 1945, an important provision called for a state tax of 1 per cent on the gross revenue of all gambling houses. During the next year this tax amounted to little more than $270,000. The tax was increased to 2 per cent, and at the same time was imposed a system of state license fees, based on the number of games operated. About the only method of gambling still banned is, as said, the lottery.

By 1952, Nevada's legal new industry paid the state $1,702,000 in direct revenue tax, plus around a third of a million dollars as its one-quarter share of the license fees paid to counties and towns. It was sufficient to estimate that the amount of money wagered on Nevada games in 1951 was more than $1½ billion.

The fact that operators of gaming houses were slow to publicize their establishments leads directly to Harold S. Smith, Sr., proprietor of Harolds Club, Reno, Nevada. This is without doubt the largest gambling house in the world. It has grown steadily since it was opened, in 1936, from a one-room shop into the present seven-story structure occupying two thirds of a city block, with offices spilling over into a second building across Douglas Alley.

Harolds Club employs 1150 people. More than one million visitors wander through the place every year. An electric eye device has counted 15,600 customers in a twenty-four-hour period. There are seven entrances, none of which is ever locked. The games include dice, roulette, chuck-a-luck, *panguingui* (commonly called pangini or "pan"), hundreds of slot machines, race-horse keno, baccarat, and twenty-one.

Let Harold Smith himself explain why other games are not offered in his club: "We don't have a racing book; if you want to bet the horses, or a sporting event, you'll have to go elsewhere. Klondike dice, or ace-away, a very popular game in the state of Washington, never caught on with our patrons so we dropped it. We also have discontinued poker, lo-ball and crapless-craps, a game in which 2 and 12 are points to be made, rather than penalties that lose your bet. We found in crapless-craps that the normal percentage of 1.41 against the player in a dice game rose abruptly to 4 per cent against him, and we don't care to gouge our customers like that. We are, furthermore, one of the few gaming houses in the world which does not employ shills to pretend-play our games when it is quiet and hope, thereby, to inspire customer action."

The three Smiths, father and two sons, who own and operate Harolds Club, have Yankee backgrounds. Daddy Raymond I. was born in Vermont, and at a tender age left the farm to run wheel games at county fairs to help support his widowed mother. His son Raymond was born, in 1907, in Burlington, Vermont, and son Harold S. was born in Denver, in 1910.

The boys attended several schools, kindergarten in Albany, New York, the early grades in Vergennes, Vermont, and later parochial and high schools in Buffalo and Cleveland. Meanwhile, the parents were divorced. The boys continued to move around a good deal, helping their father to operate the concessions he had with carnivals and at amusement parks. For a time they ran bingo games, and penny-roulette wheels in Modesto, California, and Portland, Oregon. Both games were technically illegal in those states, and the Smiths were fined now and then on gambling charges. Reform was in the air, except in Nevada. The Smiths were weary of it. They moved to Reno where, on an investment of $500, they opened in a cubbyhole between two bingo parlors in a walk-up hotel. They weren't going to compete with the parlors, but installed only the penny-roulette wheel. It was February 23, 1936, which happened to be Harold Smith's twenty-sixth birthday.

Although the one-room club was loaded with customers on its first night, the place lost $2000 in its first year. The Smiths added "twenty-one" tables, put a poker game in the back, tried ace-away, lo-ball, crapless-craps, and even Chinese fan-tan. During 1937 and 1938, it was still nip-and-tuck. The real break came with introduction of what is remembered as the mouse roulette game. Of all the many legends about Harolds Club this is the one that has become a part of western folklore. It has many versions, but let son Raymond Smith tell it in his own words: "Mother Providence seemed so fond of her babes in the gaming woods she almost laughed aloud at times. There was, for example, the incident of the mouse game. My dad has always been a pushover for strangers with exotic schemes. This one arrived one day when I was out of town. I returned to discover Daddy had hired the man and his game for $100 a week.

"The mouse game is actually a form of roulette using a live mouse as the ball. The creature is placed in a box on a table top in which are numbered holes large enough for him to crawl into. There is a drawer under the table to recapture the mouse when he drops through a hole. Each hole is numbered—ours ran from 1 to 50—and the player places his bet on the number he thinks the mouse will choose. The box is lifted and Brother Mouse makes his run. Winners are to be paid off at the same odds as roulette.

"I had spotted a version of the mouse game when I first worked concessions in Florida. No one was winning. I soon saw why. When the box was lifted the mouse would edge out, sniffing nervously at holes. Any noise or quick motion sent him scurrying down the nearest hole. The operator watched closely. He kept quiet while the animal approached holes on which players had bets. When the mouse sniffed a hole on which no money was riding the operator would wave an arm and shout:

'Anybody for a Coke?' And, zip! Mr. Mouse was down that hole.

"After the winless players departed, the operator invited me to play. I declined, pointing out I had no chance to win. He smiled and acknowledged I'd figured it right. And here, years later, I return to Reno to find this clip game in my own club!

"But Daddy was only mildly appalled. The game intrigued him even after I demonstrated it couldn't be protected for the house *or* customer. He insisted on letting the man work out his week. And now there happened a fantastic thing. Somebody took photographs of the game. News picture services sent them across the United States, with stories of the roulette played at Harolds Club with mice. The publicity brought curious crowds from far and near. Harolds Club suddenly has a wide reputation as the casino that "started from a mouse roulette game."

It was one of those things, unplanned, unthought of, that strike the public fancy. "Twenty-five years later," says Raymond Smith, "people still ask to see the mouse roulette game and won't believe that it was here only one week." Though Mr. Smith may not know it, that mouse roulette legend is often cited as the chief reason Harolds became the outstanding gambling club in all Nevada.

In any event, in the early months of 1941, Harolds Club began to boom. It was as if California had suddenly awakened to the fact of legal gaming in Reno. (Las Vegas was still nothing.) People came pouring over the mountains with their money. Harolds Club was already the biggest place, and it grew bigger almost by the hour. More games, more slots. And the Smiths weren't happy with Nevada's reluctance to promote its legal gaming. They started building enormous billboards—HAROLDS CLUB OR BUST, RENO, NEVADA—that were to blur and dazzle the eye from (unfortunate) locations within 500 miles in four directions. (As of 1961, there are 2500 of these affronts to the eye scattered, as Harold Smith likes to brag, "over much of the civilized world.")

By the time Harolds Club was virtually forced, by the pressure of expanded business, to erect the seven-story building that now houses its bars, restaurants, and gaming rooms, other professional gamblers, both local and elsewhere, were expanding too; and the city of Reno, once known only for its divorce industry, had become famed as the Gambling Capital of the World. And gambling in Nevada had by no means reached its peak.

Down at the other end of the state, Las Vegas had been stirring. As of 1962, what is called the Las Vegas Strip has grown so fast, and in such elegance, as to challenge Reno's right to call itself the Gaming Capital. (*Gaming* seems gradually to be supplanting *gambling* as a sort of long-hair description of the same industry.) Yet Reno is much the older place, and its very name has for generations been synonymous with Divorce, which is possibly why a majority of tourists include Nevada in their itinerary of travel in the West.

In writing about Reno, Lucius Beebe, one of the most widely known characters in Nevada, remarked that "there is an element in the city known as the see-our-schools-and-churches group," which deplores Reno's fame for its glittering night life, and is quick to buttonhole visiting firemen, especially writers, with entreaties to depict Reno as a normal, wholesome American community: Tell the world about the University of Nevada's ever growing enrollment, or the swelling deposits in the quarter-of-a-billion-dollar First National Bank; but forget Harolds Club and the nocturnal traps that flourish, raw and neon-lit, in town and for miles on US 395 and South Virginia Road.

Mr. Beebe thinks the schools-and-churches group fails to understand that these conventional qualities are a commonplace elsewhere in the land and that people do not come to Nevada to see more of the same. "They visit Reno," he says, "to get away from precisely these things and to find a relaxed, uninhibited way of life. They find it, too, which is just as well. Without the tourist trade, Nevada would soon be bankrupt."

If Reno people choose to doubt the Beebe thesis, he cites the experience of Reno's quite elegant Holiday Hotel. Opened some five years ago, with no gambling on the premises, save for

25. A ranger naturalist shows his party an ice crevasse on Grinnell Glacier, Glacier National Park.

26. Trick Falls is in Two Medicine Valley, in Glacier National Park.

27. Montana's beauty is a wild and rugged beauty. Between the Bitterroots and the Rockies are vast expanses of breath-taking mountains, woods, and water. (*Makoshika State Park, near Glendive, Montana*)

28. (*Glacier National Park*)

A fifty-mile stretch of Going-to-the-Sun Highway, which cuts across the rugged middle of Glacier National Park, has become one of the most greatly admired pieces of scenery in Montana.

29. More than 700,000 visitors come to Glacier National Park each year, over 98 per cent by car. (*Logan Pass, Glacier National Park*)

30. Virginia City, the first incorporated town in Montana, is second to none in restoration of ghost towns in the West. (*Virginia City, Montana*)

31. Of all the far western states, it may be said best of Wyoming that its history can be told in terms of grass . . . bluestem, buffalo grass, slough grass, bunch grass—the great grass that rippled to the horizon like a green ocean. (*Sunrise on Mt. Moran, Grand Tetons*)

32. "Black" bears, which may be either black, brown, or cinnamon colored, are the most common species found in Yellowstone National Park.

33. Pilot Peak is located on the Wyoming-Montana border just east of the northeast entrance to Yellowstone Park. It may be seen from Beartooth Highway.

34. Grand Teton National Park includes the incomparable Jackson Hole. The park has several glacial lakes; Jenny Lake is shown in the photo above.

35. In the matter of natural scenic attractions Wyoming is one of the most fortunate regions in all the West. Yellowstone National Park, in its north-eastern corner, features Old Faithful geyser.

36. Tower Falls, 132 feet high, is on Tower Creek just before it empties into the Yellowstone River.

37. The Snake River, with the Teton Range in the background, winds through the Jackson Hole country.

38. Although Arizona is one of the larger states, the tourist is seldom far from some natural wonder. This sandstone formation is near Window Rock, the Navaho Indian capital.

39. The majestic saguaro cactus, giant of the desert, is the commanding desert landmark.

40. Massive logs in the Petrified Forest National Monument are prehistoric in origin.

41. Much of the Grand Canyon is in Arizona, which properly is its official mail address. Of this vast geographic feature, it has been said that "it is probably the greatest shock ever experienced by man."

42. The Painted Desert is one of the beauty spots to be found along Highway 66 as it winds its way across northern Arizona.

43. The $125 million Hoover Dam is one of man's greatest engineering achievements. In addition to its production of power, it provides the Lake Mead National Recreational Area.

slot machines, "which nobody in Nevada considers games of chance, anyway," the Holiday advertised itself as a place where visitors who disapproved of gambling wouldn't have to encounter it. And a result, "patrons stayed away in droves; and even visitors who didn't gamble, it quickly appeared, wanted the cheerful twenty-four-hours-a-day tumult of a casino around them."

Well, the point having been proved to the satisfaction of everybody, except the schools-and-churches group, the Holiday was reopened with games of chance past counting. "You have to fight your way through the customers happily rolling snake-eyes and pushing chips onto green in the Holiday casino."

Although Mr. Beebe is now a columnist on the San Francisco *Chronicle,* his legal residence is still Virginia City, where for a decade he owned and published the *Territorial Enterprise,* a weekly newspaper dedicated to reviving the long faded hamlet and making it into the prosperous and most widely known ghost town in the Far West.

One reason Las Vegas delayed getting into the gambling boom after legalization in 1931, was that construction was just starting on the Boulder Dam, which was to cost more than $200 million of federal funds. Las Vegas stood at the closest point where connection could be made with a mainline railroad. Population skyrocketed out of sight. Even after the government built Boulder City, to house its thousands of employees, the Las Vegas boom continued. The government town forbade sale of liquor and operation of gambling houses, and each weekend saw crowds of workers hurrying into town to drink and play.

New clubs were opened along Fremont Street—the Boulder, the Frontier, the Las Vegas, the Westerner, the Monte Carlo, the Pioneer. And some of the most startling neon signs ever seen went up in the desert. When two solid blocks of Las Vegas had been filled with gaming clubs, and casino-hotels, it was obvious that more room was needed; and the Hull interests, operators of a hotel chain, bought sixty acres of sand and sagebrush on Highway 61, three miles south of town, and on it started building an elaborate tourist resort, complete with gaming casino, swimming pool, and dozens of guest cottages. This was opened as El Rancho Vegas. It was the right idea, but a bit in advance of its time. For more than a year the swanky cottages remained vacant. The property passed to new owners.

Then came the boom. Los Angeles began a thoroughgoing vice cleanup. Scores of old-time gambling joints were closed and padlocked. Thousands of Angelenos looking for action suddenly thought of Nevada. The cottages of El Rancho Vegas filled to capacity, and other big-time operators started to buy and build on what has since been known as the Las Vegas Strip. Among them was a Benjamin (Bugsy) Siegel from New York, promoter of the Flamingo, third of the Strip group, that now captured national attention when Bugsy was rubbed out in good gangland style.

It was the first major gangster killing in the region, as Oscar Lewis has pointed out, and "it revealed to Nevadans the degree to which outsiders had moved in on the theretofore largely home-owned and home-controlled gambling industry of the state." As more and more facts about Siegel came to light, it became apparent that he had a close tie with notorious crime syndicates on both East and West coasts. "The news was read in Las Vegas with something akin to consternation."

Yet, the gangland slaying in no way slowed down activities on the rapidly expanding Strip. It may have had the opposite effect. It made Las Vegas and the late Bugsy's five-million-dollar Flamingo Hotel known to millions who would otherwise have remained unaware of their existence. The tourist trade picked up amazingly. First of the post-Siegel era to open was the Thunderbird, a comparatively unpretentious establishment costing a modest $2 million.

Others were rising from the desert floor; the Desert Inn, on 170 acres, has 400 rooms, 18 holes for golf, a health club and solarium, two main dining rooms, cocktail bars, a night club, and a casino that in size and luxury has few rivals anywhere. The Desert Inn has returned a handsome profit from the day it opened. Its bars cleared $90,000 during its first month. How much its bank of slots and rows of craps and roulette and blackjack tables earned during the same period must be left to the imagination. Nevada's casino owners are no help in these matters. It is known, however, that on its opening night, some $750,000 was wagered. By figuring the average house percentages of all the games at a conservative 4 per cent, Mr. Lewis sums up, the casino's profit on its first night of play topped $30,000.

During the Desert Inn's first year of operation, it moved into first place among all Las Vegas resorts in the total amount wagered at its tables, edging out the downtown Golden Nugget, which had long held that distinction, and "so becoming second only to Harolds Club."

Two more places were opened on the Strip in 1952–53, the Sahara and the Sands; and in 1955 no fewer than three grand openings in a single month were announced. The launching of the Sahara had an unusual happening. Although the opening-night play at its tables was brisk and the bets high, luck ran consistently against the house and the casino ended its first twenty-four hours some $50,000 in the red. It was the best publicity money could buy. Before the end of the week the Sands had recouped its losses.

Today, the hundreds of thousands of wheel-happy Americans, who visit Nevada every year are likely to remind natives and long-time residents that these tourists are much like the Forty-niners, in that they are on their way to California. It is true that the average tourist of today plans to see either Reno or Las Vegas and be gone.

The rare one may want to see Ely, Winnemucca, Austin; and to visit the Mackay School of Mines at the University, in Carson City. He will probably plan his trip to include Virginia City, the "Queen of all Ghost Towns," and even the remnants of Searchlight, Rhyolite, and other places.

But outlanders have heard so much about gambling and gamblers along with the spectacular hotels and inns, and the lights, and the twenty-four-hour life of the casino streets, that they are properly conditioned as Nevada tourists the moment they cross the state line.

If the tourist crosses the state on a hot, cloudless day, and his shirt is sticking, and his temper is short, he will speak of it as a region he should just as soon never see again; as having more space with less in it than any place he has ever known. He will speak of the few stopping places, and of the frightening distances between them. He will also, probably, make the old, worn, heartfelt observation—about giving it all back to the Indians, but pity the noble redskin . . .

The native or longtime Nevadan will likely grin and agree. He is fully aware of the state's discomforts and shortcomings. If he himself is not quite content with life in what some Nevadan described as the Biggest Jukebox in the World, he is prepared to permit his sources of prosperity to say what they will about the Sagebrush State, whose area contains 110,540 square miles, and in population still ranks as forty-ninth.

MONTANA

Chapter Seven

Many years ago, in an effort to describe the then third largest state, a writer said that Montana was High, Wide, and Handsome. To certify these qualities he felt need to compare it with three others. Colorado, he wrote, is high, having more peaks than any other state. Wyoming is wide, with the breadth of the plains between the Big Horns and the Grand Tetons. California is handsome, with the splendor of success. It takes all three adjectives, said naturalist Donald Culross Peattie, to do justice to Montana.

It is a happy, pat phrase. There is much truth in it. Much of Montana is a high plateau, 3000 feet and more above the sea. From east to west it ranges some 650 miles. The "handsome" is, of course, a matter of opinion, but my own is fairly high. A famous American artist, Joseph Pennell, called Montana "the most pictorial place in America."

Montana's beauty is a wild and rugged beauty. Between the Bitterroots and the Rockies are vast expanses of breath-taking mountains, woods, and water. East of the Great Divide is some of the most ghastly terrain in America. Montanans appear to love it all, even when they can stand it no longer and move away for good to resume, in their new home, their bragging about the "grandest state in the Union" and its "damnedest weather ever seen."

Riding a transcontinental train west across the state, the outlander will likely remember a great deal of what he sees as a dreary waste. Here and there, at long intervals, a few boxlike buildings cluster around a huge grain elevator, and a grim little depot. Shoddy false fronts proclaim GENERAL STORE and SALOON. If it is summer, the sun blazes down on these pitiful shacks, baking the shingles, curling the tar paper, cooking the ground, making the rails blur as far as the eye can reach. Even the few people look parched, wind-beaten. If it is winter, the frost on the train windows may well be so thick the traveler will see nothing at all.

By the time the traveler by train is entering the Rockies, he will have seen so much emptiness as to prompt the question: *Where* do Montanans live? They live here in the mountain country, the far western quarter of the state, or at least the people in this region "seem to be thicker" than is the case east of the Great Divide.

Montana is the largest segment of the northern Great Plains, and is thus one of the eight so-called Desert States. A native has written of his state that it is at once mountainous and flat, hot and cold, beautiful and terrible, and benign and benevolent. Its problems to a large extent are typical of the region. When the pioneer had passed the one-hundredth meridian, he encountered a new land. Here was no humid, gently rolling, forested area, but a place of "vastness, semiaridity, and implacably unpredictable weather."

For years on end, while emigrants hurried on to the soft mild climate of the Northwest coast, or headed for gold in California, the very facts of geography sealed off this great and resistant northern pocket that seemed to have nothing to offer either to the settler or the adventurer. Montana waited in this vague hinterland. It was made a territory in 1864, and became a state in 1889. Yet 150 years later, according to the late Joseph Kinsey

Howard, Montana was still pretty much a vague hinterland to the average eastern seaboard citizen.

"In 1940," wrote native historian Howard, "a Boston shop clerk who was arranging to have a purchase mailed to my home in Great Falls, population 30,000, asked me if Montana had regular mail service . . . And months after United States Army Engineers began construction of Montana's $100 million Fort Peck Dam, a New York firm supplying some equipment on contract, asked New York headquarters of the Army, how to address its shipment and was told there was no such place as Fort Peck." It had been "abandoned in the 1880s . . ."

Howard believed that such ignorance of his native state prevailed in large part because Montana was a "subject colony," a captive empire of out-of-state corporations, like the Anaconda Copper Mining Company, commonly known locally as the Big Snake. Although agreeing in substance with Howard, another native historian, K. Ross Toole, blames nature, and not the evil designs of men for the fact that Montana was saddled with a colonial economy. Every one of its salient industries has been extractive. From beaver through beef to copper, "the object of men had to be to trap it, shoot it, mine it, and get out."

The capital required for frantic exploitation, whether of furs, cattle, silver, copper, or lumber, had to come from the East; and as eastern capital flowed westward, control and the bulk of the wealth flowed eastward. "It is simple," says Toole, "to point out the profligate waste of Montana's natural resources—to list the crashing blunders of haste, the blindness and shortsightedness of businessmen, and the venality of politicians. Upon reflection, however, it is not so simple to point out alternative routes that would have been more practical."

What are you going to do, in a formidable land more than a thousand miles from the centers of trade and commerce, with things like timber and copper? You cannot utilize them slowly and without waste. There was no time for contemplation, nor a place for the fainthearted. Those who invested in the ventures that made Montana what it is, took great risks. We have no list of the thousands who lost. It is easy enough to criticize the methods of the comparatively few who won.

As almost invariably the case in the Northwest, Lewis and Clark passed through parts of present Montana on their way to and from their farthest goal on the Northwest coast. Soon after the explorers reached St. Louis on their return, Manuel Lisa, a trader, took an expedition up the Yellowstone to the mouth of the Big Horn, where he established Montana's first trading post. He sent John Colter to trade with Indians at the forks of the Missouri. Colter took it upon himself also to explore what became Yellowstone National Park. The natural wonders he reported to have seen there caused that region to be called Colter's Hell and gave Colter the reputation of the "biggest liar in all the West." He was in his grave before other explorers hailed him as a truthful man who had in no manner exaggerated what he had seen: "A place where the earth boiled under your feet . . . where spouts of hot water as tall as a flagpole came roaring out of the trembling ground, and whole valleys steamed with stinking fumes, as if the lid over Hell itself had been shot full of holes . . ."

Manuel Lisa's trading post was not to stand alone for long. David Thompson came down from Canada to build Kootenai House, then Salish House, and made several trips in the Flathead country. These things presaged arrival of two British concerns, the Northwest Company and the Hudson's Bay Company, which soon merged under style of the latter; and Americans operating variously as Pacific Fur, Rocky Mountain Fur, and American Fur companies were in the field, competing for pelts. Of the more than a score of Montana trading posts established during this era, Fort Benton became the most famous. It stood at the head of navigation on the Missouri, was the point of debarkation during the gold-rush period, and survives to the present day as one of the most popular "tourist attractions." It wasn't much of a fort, nor did it need to be. It is sufficient to know that for a brief time it was occupied by the Seventh Cavalry, Montana's incomparable heroes of the Little Big Horn battle.

The nature of the fur trade began to change in the 1830s. The silk hat had appeared, and very soon the demand for beaver was falling off. The white hunters were gradually finding buffalo hides easier to obtain. The Indians noticed that the mountain streams seemed to present fewer dams than before. (In one winter, along the Marias River, a trader named Kipp had taken no fewer than 4000 pelts. Nothing to approach it was ever seen again.)

Perhaps the chief contribution of the fur trade was in exploration. For some forty years hunters, traders, and trappers had been on the move, searching out the last branch of the uppermost fork of Montana streams. When the business petered out, nearly all of this inhospitable land had been traversed and mapped. Indeed, many places discovered by the trapper were forgotten, only to be rediscovered later by emigrants in covered wagons.

On the Indian himself the fur trade was profound in its destructiveness. The white trappers brought him smallpox, for which he had no more tolerance than he did for alcohol. The very trade itself was based on alcohol. In a little while, the numbers of the Blackfeet were reduced by more than half.

One after the other, the trading posts fell into disuse, and many of them rotted where they stood; but a few remained in various conditions of decay to serve as stores at gold camps, when that mania came, as it did soon enough, to bury the few scattering remains of the fur era.

With the closing of the trade in pelts, Montana was to be comparatively somnolent for two decades, the forties and fifties. That the white man had not yet altered the aspect of Montana seems agreed. And now there was a pause of twenty years, during which, as historian Toole has pointed out, "the wealth of the land lay hidden by the land's own formidable ramparts."

Joseph K. Howard credits a John White with making the first really effective gold strike—the discovery which, like James Marshall's in California, started things going. The time was July 1862. The place was Grasshopper Creek, a tributary of the Beaverhead River. The first gold camp arose on the spot as Bannack.

Though Bannack was to be named Montana's first capital and was the site of the first territorial legislative session, the urgent prospectors could not wait; they boiled over and began chasing up and down neighboring gulches, including Alder Gulch where in 1863, a richer strike had been made. In Alder Gulch, the swarming miners voted to call their new camp Varina, in honor of the wife of Jefferson Davis, President of the Confederacy; but a federal judge refused to accept this Rebel tribute in his court records. By judicial fiat, he changed the name to Virginia City, thus bedeviling for all time the like-named towns in Nevada and Montana.

By midwinter of 1863, Virginia City had several hundred crazed prospectors. By spring the number was nearer 1000. Late that year, the cluster of camps in and near Alder Gulch could muster 6000 people and a couple of men were on the way with a printing press, to start the first newspaper in what, during 1864, became Montana Territory. The sheet was the *Montana Post*.

Rumors of gold in other districts begat new rushes. One, in the Prickly Pear Valley, christened Last Chance Gulch, turned out big. The discoverers, Stanley and Cowan, appear to have been methodical men. Before the horde had time to arrive on the scene, the two men had drawn up a code of regulations for the camp, and were ready to call a meeting to ratify the sensible rules for protection of claims, to plat a townsite, determine the size of lots, and even to name the gold camp. It was to be Helena.

No such orderly progress had been visited on Virginia City.

Its first year had seen a yield of at least $10 million in gold. The booming camp was on the way to a population of 10,000, and it had attracted what events indicate to have been a strikingly generous percentage of particularly evil men. Among these characters was Henry Plummer.

Because few if any characters have been more written about than Henry Plummer, chief of the Plummer Gang, he must have mention here, if only to preclude the complaints of Montanans, shocked that their entry in the All-America Jesse James Sweepstakes has been ignored.

Little is known of Plummer's early years, save that when he arrived in Montana, circa 1862, he enjoyed a bad record in California, Nevada, and Idaho. Apparently he had a natural charm and his obvious appeal was such as to get him elected sheriff at Bannack, and also to attract as hardy and ruthless a crew of criminals as the West could offer. In the busy ninety-mile stretch between Bannack and Alder Gulch, these highwaymen began to operate, systematically, as Plummer directed, on gold-laden coaches and individuals. That they were playing for keeps is evident. The record indicates that 102 men were their victims.

After a particularly cold-blooded murder in 1864, George Ives was arrested, not by Sheriff Plummer, but by a group of miners, who tried Ives on the spot and promptly hanged him. The execution was praised by a mass meeting in the camp; and many suggested the hanging committee be enlarged and take needed action on other candidates suspected of robbery. It was done. Forty-five miners, all members of the Masonic order, organized themselves as a vigilante committee. During less than a month, ending January 11, 1864, the vigilantes hanged twenty-four men, said to have comprised the Plummer Gang and, for good measure, added eight more ruffians. The road between Alder Gulch and Bannack not only was safe; the corrective influence of the vigilantes was felt elsewhere in Montana gold camps. Many of the vigilantes went on to become leaders in territorial and state affairs.

The wiping out of the Plummer Gang hardly interrupted the

gold excitement in Montana. A strike at Montana Bar was a sensation for several months. Another, on Silver Bow Creek, boomed for five or six years but petered out and by 1870 was all but deserted. In 1875, however, Bill Farlin opened some astonishing veins of silver in his Travonia mine, in what had long since been named Butte City and was known as a gold camp. It would soon be known, for a few years, as a silver camp, for Farlin sold his Travonia hole to W. A. Clark, who put up a stamp mill and refinery, and Butte camp grew famously to 3000 people.

Now came to Butte, from Nevada's Comstock, an experienced mine boss, Marcus Daly, who bought a small silver mine, the Alice, and erected a stamp mill. Butte grew again. Near the Alice was a shallow hole which its owner, Mike Hickey, had christened Anaconda. Daly liked the looks of this silver mine, too, and bought it from Hickey, while Daly organized the Anaconda *Silver* Mining Company before he discovered it contained a copper seam fifty feet wide. Unsuspected by himself, Daly now owned what proved to be the richest copper property the world had known.

Clark had meanwhile bought several more Butte properties classed as copper producers, and became the first of Montana's fabled copper Kings. Daly shut down his Anaconda, and let the word get around that he had been bilked. Then he quietly bought up all the adjacent claims as they were thrown on the market, and thus became the second of the Copper Kings. The third of these characters arrived a bit later. He was Frederick Augustus Heinze, Brooklyn born of a Connecticut Yankee mother and a German father. It is of interest to know that young Heinze was also a graduate of the Columbia School of Mines.

Now that the three principals had assembled on the stage, the great drama of the War of the Copper Kings could begin. Daly, Clark, and Heinze. These were the Kings. Before they were done fighting, Butte had become the Richest Hill on Earth, Montana was a sovereign state, and Montanans even had time enough to look around themselves, to discover that they lived in a country second to none in the category described as High, Wide, and Handsome.

This new appreciation of Montana by Montanans began in 1910, when more than a million acres of the public domain was set aside as Glacier National Park, and its proprietors got the feeling of a sense of being host to this immense piece of outdoors along the Continental Divide. A few years later, Canada's Waterton Lakes National Park and Glacier were merged to form what is known officially as the Waterton-Glacier International Peace Park.

Although the United States and Canadian customs still operate at the border within the parks, both appear to have agreed that the less fuss caused to tourists, the better it is for both nations. This international feature has been most effective in attracting more visitors than was the case before the co-operative courtesy became official. The very place names probably give a sense of foreign travel to visitors. Americans like to sail on Canada's Lake Waterton, "through the Bosporus to the Dardanelles," and may even enjoy staying at the Prince of Wales Hotel. Canadians may well wonder who or what Mount Oberlin is named for, but will likely take it for granted that Mount Cleveland honors a President of the United States. (N.B. Although it just happens that there is no glacier in the Canadian, or Alberta, side, there are several in the Montana part, as attested to by the Many Glacier Hotel.)

Montana may have been slow at first to appreciate the many new things in which, in a way of speaking, it had a vested interest. But as the mining industry in the eastern part of the state began to taper off, and what was not yet called the "tourist business" became suddenly evident, dude ranches and motels took on a new status. Visitors from "back East" would actually pay money to look at "out West."

It was a startling thing. For decades Montanans had known that strangers would come many miles just to see the place where

General George A. Custer made his last stand on the Bighorn River in the southeastern part of the state. They had been coming to look almost since the day of the battle (June 25, 1876) and in increasing numbers since 1886, when the federal government declared a mile-square area to be a national cemetery, and set up a monument of sandstone surrounded by an iron fence, to mark the dead. This was comprehensible to the average American, but that Americans would pay to see a mere glacier —a "mess of ice on a side hill"—was beyond understanding.

But these Custer Men who have been coming to the Monument for seventy-six years, and are known as Custer Bugs, have at last broken down. Once they have paid homage to the peerless military hero of the West—all of the West—they now tend to move on to see what other things Montana has to offer. Even glaciers.

Glacier National Park has been described as an ice-carved citadel of beauty. This high country was obviously too rugged for homesteaders, who of course paid it no heed. It was just as obviously no place for miners. To these people it was "wasteland" until it occurred to somebody who really enjoyed wasteland to give it to the government.

On the map, the park looks deceptively small, compared with Montana. Yet one is glad to know it is actually "one third as big again as Rhode Island," which doesn't mind in the least. It is probable that few if any states have been changed more by inclusion of a national park than has Montana. In addition, there is also in this state one of the five entrances to Yellowstone.

A fifty-mile-stretch of Going-to-the-Sun Highway, which cuts across the rugged middle of Glacier National Park, has become one of the most admired pieces of scenery in Montana. It had been blasted through the long "lost" Marias Pass that was discovered by John F. Stevens, James J. Hill's notable chief engineer, who was responsible for putting the Great Northern Railway through the Pacific Northwest to Seattle. In grateful recognition of this service, the railway placed, near Summit, a heroic statue of Stevens, easily seen by passengers on the north side of the tracks.

Before the highway was built, a motorist who wanted to cross the park had to ship his car over the pass by rail, or detour some 500 miles by way of Great Falls and Missoula. More than 700,000 visitors come to Glacier every summer. Over 98 per cent came by car last year.

Going-to-the-Sun Mountain and the highway at its base perpetuate the legend of Napi. He was the Old Man of the Blackfeet, which is to say, the Creator who, when his work was finished, set out for his home in the sun. He climbed the mountain, then disappeared amid swirling snows and flashes of lightning. When the sun burst forth, the Indians saw his profile engraved in rock and filled with snow. His face may still be seen on the far side of the 9604-foot peak, looming above Logan Pass.

Not in the park, yet holding a secure place among Montana's tourist lures, is Virginia City, the first incorporated town in Montana and its second territorial capital. In spite of its meager population these late times, it has managed for ninety-eight years to preserve its lurid memories, complete with a Boothill Cemetery, and a carefully catalogued collection of old records and relics. Indeed, Virginia City, Montana, is second to no restoration of ghost towns in the West. Among these reminders are the Wells Fargo Express Office, the Bale of Hay Saloon, and a company of seasoned actors who produced period melodrama during the summer season at the Stone Barn Playhouse.

Another offbeat attraction of note is the Charles M. Russell Gallery and Studio in Great Falls, which honors one of the West's greatest painters, the Cowboy Artist, whose portrayal of early days of the range, and allied scenes, has been the subject of national acclaim for many years.

In Jefferson Canyon are the Lewis and Clark Caverns, second in size to Mammoth Cave in Kentucky and the Carsbad Caverns in New Mexico. Discovered in 1902 by a surveyor, Daniel Morrison, who began alone to equip the spot with stairways long before the government saw fit to declare it a national monument, this reminder of the Lewis and Clark Expedition is one of several in the state, including Pompey's Pillar, near Billings, said to have been named because of Indian smoke signals seen there.

Mountain climbing, tramping, dude-ranch outings, together with some of the finest fishing in the United States, including Montana's own Georgetown Lake, attracts thousands of dedicated anglers who range over the state from the Madison River, said to hold the reputation of being *the* outstanding trout stream in the United States, to the locally famous Gallatin, Jefferson, Big Hole, and Beaverhead rivers.

Montana's leading industry, copper, is also still one of the state's oldest as well as most reliable tourist attractions, what with the vast smelter at Anaconda, and the world's tallest stack, which rises 585 feet. Guided tours to this and other smelters, along with visits to Butte's deep mines, and newer pits, and still newer Block Caving operations, offer a continuous show most popular with tourists. So, too, is the Montana School of Mines, at Butte, where visitors are urged to see the unmatchable museum of minerals.

WYOMING

Chapter Eight

Of all the far western states, it may be said best of Wyoming that its history can be told in terms of grass. The Sioux followed the buffalo, the buffalo followed the grass, and the settlers came to dispose of the buffalo and to send the Indians back to reservations in the Dakotas.

Bluestem, buffalo grass, slough grass, bunch grass—the great grass that rippled to the horizon like a green ocean.

For almost eighty years, the Sioux and the buffalo had kept inviolate a green strip of country along the banks of Wyoming's Powder River. It stretched 150 miles north and south, 35 miles wide from east to west, between the Big Horns and the Powder; between the North Platte in Wyoming and the Rosebud in Montana.

When the cattlemen came, time began to move faster. For less than a decade they permitted themselves to live the feudal, pastoral life that we associate with cattlemen in Texas and Southern California. This was partly their own fault; they lived too largely and too carelessly. Or so said one of them, the late Struthers Burt, head of the Bar B. C. Ranch, who wrote that Wyoming cattlemen talked far too much about their large and easy profits.

Rancher Burt summed it up: "The Powder River country was

opened to settlement in 1878. Within five years the grass was being crowded."

Blizzards took their toll. Speculation ruined others. Rustlers working on the flanks of the herds grew powerful. Overgrazing narrowed and killed the range. Then came the "nester," the homesteader, that "tragic, too big familied, running-nosed character." Then came the sheepmen, and the farmer followed, "plowing up the soil and the grasses that held it down, stirring the alkali to the surface, spreading it by irrigation. Still the cattleman survived. He alone, besides the sheepman and the horseman, was where he belonged . . ."

Today's tourist, in the 1960s, will find that the cattlemen still loom large in Wyoming, and so does the grass. There are more than 150 varieties of grass. But what might well be described as the "working" forage are the blue grasses, the wheat grasses, the fescues, and the redtops. These are enough to make a man's heart stand still, according to boosters of the state where the Great Open Spaces are said to occupy 99.9 per cent of what one is looking at.

Compared with certain other states that have been completely transformed during the past fifty years, such as Texas and California, Wyoming is basically much as it was in 1900. Only 320,000 people were counted in Wyoming's 97,000 square miles in 1958. On a reporter's visit there, Hamilton Basso remarked that most towns were from thirty to fifty miles apart, and that he had driven one hundred Wyoming miles without seeing a single habitation—or indeed, a single thing. He went away to write of it that he knew of no other place where man's passage had left so little imprint on the state. "Everywhere his footprints are lost in the grass." He found it hard to escape the feeling that if Wyoming's first aboriginal inhabitants were to return today, along with the Indians who came after them, they would find the country much as they left it.

In the matter of natural scenic attractions Wyoming has been and is one of the most fortunate regions in all the West. Yellowstone National Park stands in its northeastern corner; and nearby is Grand Teton National Park, which includes incomparable Jackson Hole. There are also several national forests, of which the Big Horn is not far from the Hole-in-the-Wall, with which Wyoming's most notorious outlaws, the Wild Bunch, are identified. (George Armstrong Custer had the bad grace to fight and die not on the Big Horn River in Wyoming, but on the Little Big Horn in Montana.) Still, Wyoming isn't so badly off for heroes. There is Cody, a town named for a man, Buffalo Bill, who has been publicized more and longer than any other western American who comes readily to mind.

Wyoming's Wild West of pulp-paper literature, and of movies and television is, like the Wild West of other states, based on actuality, but distorted, foreshortened, and heightened. Struthers Burt said that this period occupied less than ten years of actual time. Wyoming has since done what it could to dramatize the legend, to keep it fresh not only for the sake of dude-ranch visitors and the swarming tourists, but also for the self-respect of natives and long-time residents. After all, the varying degrees of Wild Westernness between one state and another are matters of pride as well as business.

Twenty-five years ago the West was laughing at the ladies in "queer pants" and their male companions who wore neck handkerchiefs hind-end-to. And the West was also suspicious of those new dude ranchers who encouraged the aliens from eastern cities "to ruin horses and frighten steers." All that is changed now. There are more dude ranches than cattle ranches in any western state.

One has to bear in mind that Wyoming is at base what it has always been, a grazing state. The fact that there are nearly twenty times more domestic animals in the state than human beings sums up the situation. It is simply not the sort of place that attracts people in overpowering numbers. Well, what are those who *do* come here going to see in Wyoming, and what are they going to do? Dude ranches is one answer. Many will be content to get into pants that are now called levis, sit on the rail, swing on the gate and sing "Don't Fence Me In."

In the past three decades, Wyoming has thought up and arranged many more things to amuse the eastern city folks who like to fancy they have discovered a pocket where time was stopped many years ago, and they can live for a while in the past of the Wild, Wild West. The biggest and oldest of Wyoming's more than a score of celebrations is Cheyenne's Frontier Days whoopee, usually staged in July. Once upon a time, Cheyenne, the state's capital and most important city, enjoyed the reputation of being one of the toughest, six-gun-towns in the West. Along with Deadwood, South Dakota, and Tombstone, Arizona, it was a peerless setting for dime novels which managed to tar, or to gild Cheyenne so thoroughly with the Wild West myth, that a popular TV-Western of the 1960s is named "Cheyenne" for its star.

In its annual revival of traditions, the city devotes a week of days and nights to the glory of the cow, the horse, and the man who form the proper symbol of Wyoming. It has grown into an immense show that attracts both amateur and professional rodeo performers from all parts of the West.

Among the many other Wyoming towns which put on annual events inspired by historical figures or happenings is Cody, with its William F. Cody Day, honoring Buffalo Bill, Cody Stampede, and a Trappers Ball. Wheatland has a Days of '49 doings which, despite the name has nothing to do with the Gold Strike in California; and also a Stone Age Fair. Casper usually has a big horse show and something called Wyoming on Parade. There are rodeo affairs at Shoshoni, Big Piney, Pinedale, Saratoga, Sheridan, Dubois, Thermopolis, and Evanston.

Tourists and other prospective visitors should check with state or local authorities before making plans to attend the events named above, and also for other celebrations, such as the Old Settlers' Picnic, at Devil's Tower; the Gillette Roundup; the Lander Pioneer Days; the Jackson Hole Frontier Days, the Sho-

shone Sun Dance, at Fort Washakie; the Old Timers Picnic, Hyattville; the Mormon Pioneer Days pageants in most Mormon communities; the Laramie Jubilee; and the Wyoming State Fair at Douglas.

Of Wyoming communities, Sheridan probably has as much built-in western flavor as any town in the state. Reporter Basso especially liked the way Sheridan's commercial establishments are strung out along Main Street in "good cow-town fashion." There were a few Indians on the streets, but they had "obviously been brought up to date." No more buckskin for them. They "go around in bright blankets of modern design milled in New England." The ranch hands were dressed in cowboy garb "that a sophisticated fifth-grader would look down upon."

Geographically, Wyoming has been described as the principal height of land of the United States. It is a mountain top, all of it. Its mountain ranges are merely the tips of a single mountain. The state is twice the size of New York, thirty-eight times larger than Rhode Island, and only half as large as Montana. And because Wyoming is so high no one yet has been able to get at its minerals, it there are any. It is surrounded by great mineral-bearing states—Montana, Idaho, Utah, Colorado; and in every case mineral deposits played a large part in the exploration and settlement of those regions. Wyoming remained a place of grass, a grazing state pure and simple.

Perhaps nobody else has pointed out so graphically the advantages and shortcomings of Wyoming's geographic position as the late Struthers Burt. Long ago he wrote that "you can dodge in and out and around Wyoming hardly aware of any mountains at all." This is because "the really big mountains hide themselves." Wyoming is so high that the mountains level out and afford an easy gateway, "as if the earth were content to rest and lie down after having climbed so far." For this reason, Wyoming became the great northern route to the West Coast when, it was suddenly discovered in the 1840s, "you could take wagons straight across the southern part of the state to the Pacific."

And that is what happened. To many thousands of covered-wagon people, Wyoming was a way station on the road to Oregon and California. For many years more, few thought of actually *living* there.

The first inhabitants of record were the Crows and the Absarokas who lived in the fastnesses of the Big Horns for more years than man can know. At the northern end of the Big Horns is a relic of peoples older than the American Indians. This is known as the Medicine Wheel. It is a huge circle of stones with carefully placed boulders marking the radius of the spokes. It is probably the oldest work of man in North America. It is also virtually unknown outside Wyoming's borders. If it lay in England, it would be as famous as Stonehenge. Where it lies, 10,000 feet up a peak in the Big Horns, it can be said to be barely available, and only to the rare tourist as determined as he is courageous. The last three miles were fairly recently reported to seem more like three hundred miles of "foot-deep ruts, slithery mud, a large patch of glassy ice (it was July), abrupt curves." Unless a great deal of work has been done on this approach, the Medicine Wheel will remain a matter of hearsay to vast numbers of summer visitors to Wyoming. They will have to be content with knowing that the wheel is 70 feet in diameter and 245 feet in circumference, that its center is a mound of stones like a hub, from which twenty-eight spokes radiate to the rim of the wheel. That, and that the old men of the Crow tribe believe the wheel was there "before the light came."

After the light came, the Sioux were seen in the grass country along the Powder River. The Crows held the Big Horns. The Blackfeet and the Crows hunted over the grasslands of Montana. Then, here on the fringe of the Northwest, came Lewis and Clark, followed by hunters, trappers, and traders, who were also explorers. After them came the settler, then the railroad.

Though John Colter first appeared in western history as a member of the Lewis and Clark party, he dropped off on the way back from Oregon, to set up as a trader in company with Manuel Lisa, at a fort at the mouth of the Big Horn River in

Montana. Here in Colter is the man of whom it has been said that he discovered Wyoming practically singlehanded. As soon as he and Lisa established their post, Colter, on snowshoes, with his rifle and thirty-pound pack went forth to find the Crows and other tribes who might like to trade with the white men. On this journey, he covered some 500 miles, traveling through Yellowstone Park, where no white man had trod before, and returned in the spring to the post. The Crows had liked him.

Soon enough, he was away again, and again he passed through Yellowstone, this time to observe more closely what he *thought* he had seen on his first trip. These were the natural wonders which, as said, Colter reported faithfully and accurately, only to gain reputation as the West's biggest liar.

"Nowadays," remarks a Wyoming historian, "thousands of people go through 'Colter's Hell' every summer, and of these thousands there are still a goodly number who believe nothing . . . until bears bite them. Not believing anything until a bear bites you is a glandular deficiency, not a question of information."

As for John Colter, he ran up a string of "firsts" in Wyoming without compare. He was the first white man to see the headwaters of the Wind, the Snake, and the Green rivers; the first to see Jackson Hole and the Tetons. Not even Jim Bridger, who "got everywhere in Wyoming and knew every foot of it" had seen so many places in so brief a time as Colter.

Neither Colter nor Bridger seem to have had anything to do with the name "Wyoming." This was left to a congressman, James M. Ashley, from Ohio, who, in 1865, introduced in the House a bill "to provide a temporary government for the Territory of Wyoming." This was done, and it was admitted as a state in 1890. The name is said to derive from the Delaware Indian language and was first applied to the Wyoming Valley in Pennsylvania. It is also said to signify the western state's outstanding topographic feature, the Great Plains.

The creation of Wyoming Territory out of Dakota Territory was in one respect more important than its statehood. One of the first acts of the territorial legislature, when it convened in

1869, granted equal rights to women for the first time in America. And within a year, women were serving on juries at Laramie, and Mrs. Esther M. Morris of South Pass City was appointed the first woman justice of the peace anywhere.

National leaders of the woman suffrage movement were as startled as they were deliriously happy with the astounding action of Wyoming's territorial legislators. The whole affair had been accomplished so quietly that even such alert women as Mrs. Stanton, Miss Stone, and Miss Anthony were taken by surprise.

Observing in a formal statement that a happy life is one without a history, the three leaders remarked, rather helplessly, that because the vote had been obtained in Wyoming without agitation or strife, there was no struggle to record. Looking around, naturally enough, for a heroine, they found her in Mrs. Amelia Post who, when territorial Governor John A. Campbell hesitated to sign the bill, led a body of women of Cheyenne to his residence and announced they should stay there until he did sign. Thus, according to woman suffrage headquarters in New York, did "the magnificent Territory of Wyoming lay the foundation for the first true Republic."

Almost a year before Wyoming achieved territorial status, a melancholy event in adjacent Colorado practically guaranteed that Indian troubles would harass Wyoming—and much of the West too—for years to come. This was the Sand Creek Massacre performed by Colorado Militia under orders of the Rev. J. M. Chivington, who was also a militia colonel. In November of 1864, he and his troopers made a surprise attack on an encampment of Indians and butchered 300 of them on the spot—man, woman, child, and babe in arms.

General Nelson A. Miles, certainly no man to quail at the sight of blood, called it "the foulest and most unjustifiable crime in the annals of America." (Later writers, however, have not been either so harsh or so positive about it.)

The court-martial of Chivington was a national trial in that much of the United States was the prosecution. And for a dozen years, Indian uprisings increased all over the West, to end at the Little Big Horn when Custer, the blond, brave glory-hunter, made his last stand—and his last mistake.

The Custer fight was technically a victory for the Indians. Actually the victory was the climax of resistance, and in it was defeat. The Sioux were done. Which was to say, the redskins were done. A flurry of revolt now and then flared on the reservations. For instance: Four Sioux policemen were killed and two wounded and nine Hunkapapas fell when the government decided to arrest Sitting Bull in 1889. The great old Chief and his seventeen-year-old son also were killed in the affray.

Why fight any longer? The buffalo were going fast. The remnants of their great herds, like the Indians, were soon to be isolated on reservations. The government had permitted destruction of bison as rapidly as possible. They were the Sioux commissary. When they were gone, the Sioux would have to beg their food, like lesser tribes, from the United States.

The railroad was coming. In the spring of 1867, General Dodge located a division point on the Union Pacific at Crow Creek and called it Cheyenne. The rails were to be laid across Wyoming at top speed. By November the track layers had arrived, and their head camp, known as Hell on Wheels, was roaring day and night with the confusion of 10,000 workers and 10,000 animals, not to mention some 2000 camp followers.

The gangs were now composed of ex-Union and ex-Confederate soldiers, hundreds of Irishmen from New York, ex-convicts from everywhere, and a scattering of Great Plains mule skinners, and dubious bushwhackers. They had hardly turned up a mile of Nebraska sod, where the work began on the eastern end of the transcontinental, when a whole raft of gamblers, sellers of grog, and female harpies set up shop handy to the right of way. They or their likes were to follow the railhead until the two sections, the Union Pacific and the Central Pacific, met at Promontory, Utah, sixty miles west of Ogden.

Here in Wyoming, the construction company armed its ex-soldiers with carbines, rifles, and revolvers because—so General

Dodge had been told—the Indians wanted no rails laid across the buffalo country. But General W. T. Sherman, on a visit, said he did not think the savages would trouble a great deal. "So large a number of workmen distributed along the line," he prophesied, "will introduce enough whiskey to kill all the Indians within 300 miles of the road."

This statement turned out to be short of true prophecy. There was plenty of whiskey, to be sure, yet the Indians did not get enough of it to lay their fears. Across Nebraska, then across Wyoming, as far as Bitter Creek, the construction crews often had to drop their tools and pick up guns. The Army supplied partial protection, but the troops were too few. As General George Crook tartly observed, it was "difficult to surround three Indians with one soldier."

Across Wyoming, the railhead moved swiftly despite encounters with redskins. Out in front were the surveyors, still running lines, and staking out the route; then came the graders who, with good luck, could build about 100 miles of roadbed in thirty days. As soon as the grade was finished, the bridge crews took up their job and tried to keep some 25 miles ahead of the track-men.

Meanwhile, the railhead (or end-of-steel) moved from Cheyenne to Laramie, then to Benton, Green River, and Bear River City; and the townsites filled up with people—population—as one watched. By the time construction moved west of Wyoming's borders, it was seen that the people living between Cheyenne and Green River had "more convenient access to the capitals of Nebraska and Utah, and even of Nevada, than to Yankton in Dakota Territory." (Wyoming had been a part of Dakota Territory before its territorial status.)

Wyoming, as said, was one of the few western states that never had a real gold rush. I mean not only a commotion in the class with California's, but not even a little one like those in Oregon, Washington, Idaho, Montana, and half a dozen more including South Dakota. All of these excitements had something to do with attracting people, many of whom later became actual settlers. Wyoming had to make "progress," as population was often called, by other means. In this case, as indicated, the means were grass, and the settlers turned out to be ranchers, cattlemen.

Yet the legend of gold in the West was so powerful that in my (reproduction) copy of Rand, McNally's great Pioneer Business Atlas of the West, 1876–77, the map of Wyoming shows two mountain ranges labeled, big and bold, the BLACK HILLS. One of them is in northeast Wyoming, the other is southwest. In the spring of 1876, the Black Hills, which most maps agreed was in Dakota Territory, were fairly alive with prospectors seeking gold. Rand McNally's cartographers, busy in distant Chicago, may well have slipped a fraction of a degree of longitude.

In any event, the Black Hills were sensationally in the news in 1876. And on another page of the atlas was a big pen-and-ink sketch which readers could have thought referred to the same Black Hills so prominent on the Wyoming map.

This fanciful illustration depicts two men. One is obviously a sort of mountain man. He is all buckskinned from foot to shoulder. He carries a rifle. The other figure is an Indian, in breechclout and leggings, a tomahawk in his belt. He has one hand on the white man's shoulder. With the other arm he is pointing into the distance. Says the caption: GOLD! GOLD! BIG HEAP GOLD!

Wyoming was admitted as a state into the Union by Act of Congress on July 10, 1890. No matter the alleged gold in its legend, nor the buckskin, the rifle, the mountain man, and the Indian; the realists took over when it came to the Great Seal and Official Flag. The central figure is a woman on a pedestal. In one hand she holds a banner on which appears the legend, EQUAL RIGHTS.

ARIZONA

Chapter Nine

For many years Arizona liked to identify itself simply as the Youngest State. For half a century it had been a Territory before, in 1912, it was admitted to the Union. It is possible that citizens had tired of explaining to outlanders why it had remained so long in the pseudo-status of Frontier America.

But the freshness of the nickname wore off rather soon, and proud Arizonians looked around for an adjective that would indicate some quality of the new commonwealth to give it a little tone, something to brag about. This forced draft resulted in several suggestions, among them a couple so far-fetched—"the Italy of America" and "the Valentine State" as could have gagged all but the most frantically urgent citizens. When these were tactfully dropped, a number of replacements were proposed, like the Aztec State, the Baby State, the Sand Hill State, the Sunset State, the Apache State, the Copper State. But, according to *The World Almanac* for 1960, however, none of these nicknames made the grade. Says this all but universal authority:

ARIZONA: Grand Canyon State; Capital, Phoenix. Area: 113,909 sq. mi., rank, 6th. Population: (Census Bureau est. 1958), 1,140,000, rank, 35th. Motto: *Ditat Deus,* God Enriches. Flower: Giant Cactus or Saguaro. Bird: Cactus Wren. Tree: Foothill Palo Verde. Admission: 48th.

Much of the Grand Canyon is in Arizona, and so properly is its official mail address. Of this vast geographic feature, it has been said that "it is probably the greatest shock ever experienced by man." This puts the Grand Canyon of the Colorado in a class by itself. I am content to leave it so, better to mention lesser things which are also to be seen in this fortunate region which "God Enriches" and is publicly thanked for His bounty.

Although Arizona is one of the larger states, yet the tourist afield is seldom far from some natural wonder. They are scattered from its northern border where the Grand Canyon National Park begins, to the border of Mexico and the national monuments named Saguaro, Chiricahua, and Organ Pipe Cactus. Other government reservations include the Gila Cliff Dwellings, the Casa Grande, the Tuzigoot, Sunset Crater, Walnut Canyon, Wupatki, Tonto, the Petrified Forest, the Montezuma Castle, Canyon de Chelly, and the Navaho National Monument. Also available is the Lake Mead National Recreation Area.

In *Arizona Days and Nights*, officially the Arizona Republic's Magazine, the state is said to "produce 35 per cent of the nation's copper" . . . and it is, in fact, the largest producer of the red metal in the United States. This is in keeping with the claim more often seen and heard than is mention of the Grand Canyon.

But perhaps the most realistic description of Arizona of the 1960s is that of a gifted magazine writer, Joe Alex Morris. He called it: *Arizona: Air-conditioned Desert.*

Here is a slogan fit for the time and place. It is at once a brag of modernity, and an admission of climate and terrain which, without the brag, could well stop both industry and tourism in their tracks.

When reporter Morris asked a banker of Phoenix what was making this desert bloom with dollars, the answer was two things. "Air-conditioning and jet air travel," said the banker, and explained matters. It is really very simple: "Jet planes bring you to what until recently was an isolated state. And modern air-conditioning makes it possible for you to live through the summers after you get there." He added that in former times, "everybody who could, used to flee at the approach of summer in Arizona."

Other commentators, while citing air conditioning, are likely to mention the fact that low taxes are playing a large part in the unprecedented boom of Arizona industry. In 1950, the state repealed an inventory tax on manufactures. (More than a decade later, California still has such a law.) Arizona also reduced an oppressively heavy tax on manufacturing machinery and equipment. Phoenix and other centers have been rezoned to provide plenty of space for light industry, although no space at all for the kinds of industry that produce a lot of smoke and require an excessive amount of precious water.

One of the first things in Arizona sure to strike the visitor is the consciousness about water of citizens or all-year residents. This is of course also true of the Southwest as a region. Although Southern California seems to make more noise about scarcity of water, this may well be because it has been practicing longer than Arizona and has developed a greater volume of complaint. Yet it is generally known that the newer state's boosters are dedicated to the proposition that Arizona not only must have more water but that in some mysteriously vague manner "deserves" it.

That Arizona is going to need water to keep up with its continuing boom is obvious. Since the end of the war, an estimated six million Americans have moved westward across the United States looking for elbow room and the sun-drenched life. A great many of them have piled up along the Pacific Coast. But a lot of them got no farther than Arizona. They liked what they saw and stayed. In 1960, people there numbered 1,180,000. The Census Bureau estimated that this population will double by 1975. Nobody seems worried about future water supply. Many believe that by that time atomic energy will have supplanted hydroelectric power anyhow. Meanwhile, however, the controversy over apportioning of water from the Colorado and other streams will probably continue, and so will the strategy of the political wars in Congress.

Many Americans who never visited Arizona until the post-war boom, moved astonished into the air-conditioned desert era of the 1960s, and had to accept the region as best they could as a sort of improbable never-never land, a mirage that had somehow or other taken on the substance of reality. Where else than on a movie set does "the average citizen wake up, of a morning, in his air-conditioned home, take a dip in the swimming pool, then dress and get into his air-conditioned automobile and drive to the air-conditioned basement of his office building which, naturally, is air-conditioned? He eats in an air-conditioned restaurant, perhaps attends an air-conditioned theater. It is much the same for the man who works in an air-conditioned factory."

But air conditioning does not alone comprise the miragelike setting of so much of modern urban life in Arizona. The plush new motels of the Phoenix-Tucson area, and the glittering shops of Scottsdale—the Town Millionaires Built—form a background pattern of comfort and elegance for the desert that has now bloomed, to cite one statistic, with 10,000 tourists who spend annually some $280 million where the giant cactus grows.

It was not always thus. When our war with Mexico ended, the treaty of Guadalupe Hidalgo (1848) set the southern boundary of Texas at the Rio Grande and ceded to the United States the future states of Nevada, Utah, most of Arizona, a large part of New Mexico, parts of Colorado and Wyoming, and all of California. The southern border of New Mexico, which included present Arizona, was fixed at the Gila River. In 1853, the Gadsden Purchase acquired the strip of land between the Gila and the present boundary of Arizona and New Mexico, which was not a part of the Mexican cession. It was the last addition to the present boundaries of the United States.

Out of early government surveys came the forerunner of the

present Atchison, Topeka & Santa Fe Railroad, which crossed north-central Arizona westward from Zuni, New Mexico, to Cajon Pass, California, and has ever since played a notable part in the building of the state. By February 1863, Congress passed an act creating the Territory of Arizona, with boundaries approximately the same as today, except that they included a part of lower Nevada.

During the lengthy territorial period, Arizona experimented with seats of government. First it was at Fort Whipple, an army post; then it was Prescott, which grew up around the governor's mansion. In 1867, the capital was moved to Tucson, and ten years later was returned to Prescott, where it remained until 1889, when Phoenix became what turned out to be the permanent capital.

For almost as long, Arizona continued to have Indian troubles which, at least in retrospect, seemed to have meant the Apache tribe. The outstanding chieftains at different periods were Cochise and the later Geronimo. Things gradually quieted, and as early as 1892, a bill proposing statehood was killed in the Senate, revived in 1902, and finally passed in 1912, when it was signed by President Taft. It was the forty-eighth and last state admitted to the Union until Alaska and Hawaii came in.

Long before the possibly sobering influence of statehood could take hold of things, Arizona Territory had achieved and doubtless earned a reputation of Wild Westernness that was to make the area enormously popular with storytellers of the dime-novel School.

Indian fighters? Until well into the 1880s, Apaches were keeping much of the United States Army busy. The woolly West heyday of the cattlemen and sheepmen? This is where Zane Grey's immense cast of characters was to perform, where Colt's hardware was standard equipment.

Arizona Territory was more: in its Cochise County was immortal Tombstone, whose newspaper, bearing the name of *Epitaph,* was founded in 1880 by John P. Clum to report the all but

44. New Mexico, "the Land of Enchantment," represents a blend of three cultures . . . native Indian, Spanish, and American. (*White Sands, Alamogordo, New Mexico*)

45. New Mexico's state flower is the desert yucca, probably the most beautiful of desert vegetation. It is sometimes called Spanish Bayonet.

46. Taos Pueblo looks today very much as it did in 1540 when it was visited by an officer of Coronado's expedition. Taos is but one of the eighteen inhabited Indian pueblos in New Mexico.

47. Carlsbad Caverns (left) were established as a national park in 1930.

48. El Morro National Monument (right).

49. Each June the De Vargas Procession is re-enacted at the Palace of Governors (below) in Santa Fe.

50. Chaco Canyon National Monument includes Pueblo Bonito, the largest single ruin in the Park System, and seventeen other major pueblo ruins.

51. Bandelier National Monument, near Santa Fe, contains over 300 cliff dwellings and fascinating prehistoric pueblo ruins.

52. The oldest house in the United States, on De Vargas Alley in Santa Fe, is typical of early Santa Fe architecture, a combination of Spanish and pueblo styles and construction methods.

53. Colorado is incomparably the highest state. With 1500 peaks rising 10,000 feet or more, Colorado has a mean altitude of 6800 feet, exceeding that of any other state. High in the Crystal River country of Gunnison County is this old water-powered ore mill in the ghost mining town of Crystal.

54. The largest and most famous of the Indian cliff dwellings, about 700 years old, is the Cliff Palace in Mesa Verde National Park.

55. Melting snow on the peak of Mount Sopris, near Carbondale, provides water for the fertile valleys below.

56. A high-country lodge in Castle Valley is buried deep in winter's snow.

57. Visitors to the Black Canyon of the Gunnison National Monument (right) look more than 200 feet straight down.

58. Steamboat Springs, on the Yampa River, is a resort area of northwestern Colorado.

59. A husky-dog team passes buildings of the ghost town of Ashcroft on the way to the high, wild snow country.

60. No ghost town, but a modern mining community, Gilman is perched on the side of Battle Mountain above the Eagle River Canyon.

61. Three generations of a Navaho family pose by a half-finished rug. Their sheep graze in the background. The scene is near Phoenix, Arizona.

62. This is the Monument Valley area, where the four states of Arizona, Utah, Colorado, and New Mexico come together. The area is rich in oil and uranium, as well as the scenic beauty of red sandstone.

63. *The Territorial Enterprise,* published in this building in Virginia City, Nevada, once had a circulation greater than any other newspaper in the West. Mark Twain was one of its editors.

65. Salt Lake Temple, in Salt Lake City, Utah, is one of four Mormon temples in the state. It took forty years to build, and was completed in 1893. Baptisms, marriages, and other sacred ordinances of the Latter-Day Saints are performed here.

64. Palm Springs, California, a luxurious desert resort since the early thirties, is at the base of Mount Jacinto. Nearby Palm Canyon has an ancient grove of native palms.

66. In Cimarron Canyon, New Mexico, handsome palisades march high against the sky, extending eastward from Eagle's Nest Lake toward Cimarron.

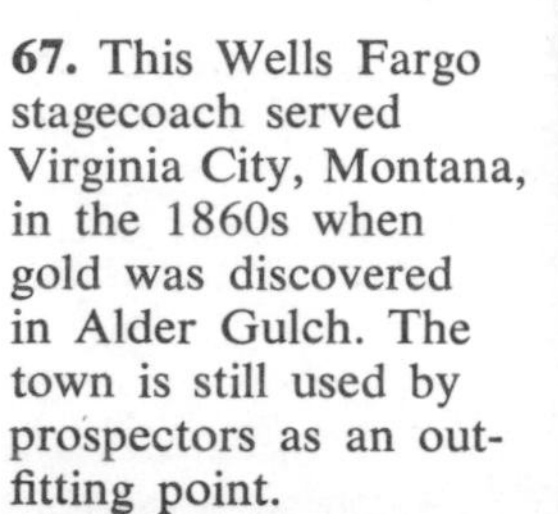

67. This Wells Fargo stagecoach served Virginia City, Montana, in the 1860s when gold was discovered in Alder Gulch. The town is still used by prospectors as an outfitting point.

incredible doings of a crew responsible for the most widely known mining town in all the West.

One should bear in mind that these and other western characters were not only popular with the dime novelists of the seventies, eighties, and nineties, but were to be worked over again and again by the writers of motion pictures and the concocters of television scripts of the present day. For ninety years many of them have been continuously familiar to millions of American readers and viewers who may have known little else about their country's background.

The Tombstone story begins with Ed Schiefflin, the desert rat from Oregon, who until 1877 was known to almost nobody. Then, in a dizzying moment he drove his pick, almost halfway to the handle, into a long streak of stuff that all but blinded him. It looked like silver, and it *was* silver.

"A feller told me," said Ed Schiefflin, "that all I'd find around here was my tombstone." And that's what he named the strike, Tombstone.

Things moved swiftly in what the press hailed as the Solid Silver Wonder Camp. Within days a couple hundred prospectors had arrived and started to file claims. Then came the saloon men, the prostitutes, the assorted hangers-on in droves.

The city of Tombstone was platted, even to a Boot Hill that was thoughtfully set aside in which to plant the casual victims incident to mining camps on the boom. Population reached about 7000 by 1881. To have called the roll at that period would have named a cast of movie and television characters still notorious eighty-odd years later:

Already at work variously as lawmen were Wyatt Earp, and brothers Morgan, Virgil, Warren, and James, a bartender; together with a psychopath called Doc Holliday. Opposing the Earps were the alleged baddies, operating as Clantons and McLowerys, and called the Cowboy Gang. All of the necessary scenery and props were available—the Wells Fargo stages, to be robbed of bullion; saloons named Crystal Palace and Oriental, whose solid, impervious bars stopped stray bullets; a Bird Cage Theater, background for gunplay that often broke out during the show; and the celebrated O.K. Corral, where the Showdown left three "outlaws" dead (two more had scrammed), and two Earps badly wounded.

As an active mining camp, Tombstone had only a decade of high production. By 1890 its population had fallen to 1875. Underground water closed many bonanzas. In 1914 the surviving properties were sold to Phelps Dodge Corporation. At that time it was estimated that some $80 million in minerals had been taken from the Tombstone mines.

As for Tombstone the town, it has become a fascinating and well-cared-for museum of a ghost town, living on its legends for a steady influx of tourists; and rousing once a year for its Helldorado Celebration, which brings thousands of visitors and includes a realistic representation of the old camp's famous moment, when the Earp boys and Doc Holliday swung four abreast along Fremont Street, heading for the O.K. Corral, and TV glory.

Not far from Tombstone is Bisbee where Phelps Dodge operates one of the biggest open-pit copper mines in the world. This monster hole has become one of the state's major tourist attractions, with grandstand seats just off a new highway, and visitors can watch modern equipment producing a good share of Arizona's annual $264 million of the red metal.

Having seen Bisbee, the modern copper mine in fullest swing, I wanted to visit Jerome, Arizona, to see what happens when a former "biggest mine" peters out. There can be few sights more melancholy. Being in the desert, nature has done nothing to hide these remnants of men's dreams. Muted conversation echoes loud in the deserted warrens of the side streets. Even the grace of weeds is denied the stark masses of mine tailings, as grim today as they were when the desperate pumps could no longer keep water from the lower levels.

These and similar thoughts crowded fast as, after a 250-mile drive from Bisbee, we entered Jerome which, in its day before 1953, had produced some $800 million in copper. We had approached by way of the Verde Valley, where we paused among the tall smelter stacks and the hush of Clarksdale, where Jerome's ore used to be treated, to gaze upward at Jerome itself. There, some 1800 feet above us, 5 miles distant, and ranged on Mingus Mountain, stood the noted copper camp, looking much as it had a decade ago, when the hoists, the railroad and the smelter stopped for good, and the population started to slide from 15,000 to its current few hundred. Tier upon tier, Jerome climbed the mountain till the top layer reached 1500 feet above the lowest. Few sights could be more unreal.

Parking near the Jerome Historical Society, I applied and was granted, for a modest $2, a membership. After a tour of the splendid museum, I took off alone on foot to see the sights.

I doubt that Gibbon himself, on another occasion, was impressed by what he saw in Rome more than I was by Jerome. Across a deep, wide gulch stood the remains of the Little Daisy Hotel, named for a mine. This really immense structure, built of stone and concrete against the stark mountain, presented a long curving panorama, three stories high, of apertures that had been windows and doors. The over-all effect is that of a veritable classic ruin, say, the Colosseum. There is nothing else like it in Arizona.

Here and there in the main business district still stood four- and five-story concrete buildings, now hollow shells, without doors, windows, or even roofs. Most stores were empty and boarded up. Street after street of homes and boarding houses were deserted. A few saloons on Main Street were operating, and two lunch counters.

I already knew that this old camp was named for Eugene Jerome of New York, one of whose daughters, Jennie, became the mother of Winston Churchill of England. For many years the operating company was United Verde Copper; then Phelps Dodge took over. In 1925 a monstrous charge of explosive started a landslide which moved things around; the city jail skidded across the highway, and it still lay on its side below street level. Several stores and the post office slipped a block or two downhill. For a few years more much of the town continued to move slowly but steadily toward the yawning valley.

Jerome's future, like many ghost camps elsewhere, probably lies in tourism. During the month (July) I was there, no fewer than 4413 visitors registered at the Mine Museum. In view of Jerome's isolation from population centers like Phoenix and Tucson, the number of visitors struck me as most encouraging. The setting itself is incomparable, the most spectacular of any old mine town I know of.

Although mining income has increased from $115 million in 1942 to $361 million in 1962; and farm income from $91 million to $385 million during the same period, according to a survey by *Fortune* magazine, it is significant that farming and mining combined, which in 1942 accounted for 73 per cent of Arizona's major sources of income, have dropped to 51 per cent. *It is the tourist and the industrialist* who have worked the change.

Arizona's tourist income today is more than $200 million. No little of this cash stems from the nostalgia inherent in scenes of the Old West of Arizona's storied past. Wyatt Earp and Cochise and assorted baddies walk and shoot again, and so does Ed (Tombstone) Schiefflin.

Manufacturing income had soared beyond the wildest expectations of local boosters: from $50 million in 1942 to $475 million in 1962. The influx was sudden. Since 1948, more than 210 new industries have located in the Phoenix area, to create 15,320 new jobs and an annual payroll of $73,500,000.

These new arrivals are known as "dry" industries, light water users; and also, because of the state's relative remoteness from markets, they are concerns making products of high value and low weight. For example: $1 million in transistors can be packed into a single truck and shipped from Phoenix or Tucson to Los Angeles overnight.

Among the several manufacturers that have moved big plants to either Tucson or Phoenix are Hughes Aircraft, General Electric, Goodyear Aircraft, Kaiser Aircraft & Electronics, and Motorama, Inc.

It is said that Arizona factories are swallowing Arizona farms. This is nothing to worry about, save for farmers. To produce a single cotton crop calls for 100,000,000 gallons of water—more than enough to support, on the same acreage, a residential-industrial complex of 2500 inhabitants.

Cotton is now grown and ginned in Arizona, shipped 2000 miles to the spinning mills, then shipped back to garment manufacturers in Phoenix and Tucson.

More water is on the way with work starting on the Glen Canyon Dam, a Bureau of Reclamation project, which within ten years will form on the Colorado River a lake 186 miles long. This should also make of the area a new playground, to add to tourist income.

It must not be supposed that, among the many fortunate advantages which both geography and other circumstances have heaped upon the state, there are no problems facing Arizonians. There is an uneasy feeling about the fact that some 14 per cent of the land is owned by the state and 71.2 per cent is owned or held in trust by the federal government. This makes a total of 85 per cent in public lands.

Many a citizen contends that more land, particularly land adjacent to the booming areas, should be opened to private ownership in order to promote economic growth and to give the state the benefit of additional taxes. Of late years this attitude has become debatable. The federal government now maintains parks, roads, dams, Indian-reservation schools, military airfields and other facilities and pays sizable amounts in salaries that constitute a favorable contribution to the state's economy. Although the subject often stirs up emotions among interested citizens, a number of highly vocal experts doubt that much of the land could be put to private use that would produce as much income as the state receives at present. One pleasant way to convert citizens to be content with the status quo of Arizona's public lands might be a subscription to *Arizona Days and Ways,* a periodical with few if any peers in the field of state magazines East or West.

NEW MEXICO

Chapter Ten

After being a territory for sixty-two years, New Mexico at last became a state of the Union on January 6, 1912. As far as continental United States is concerned, it is some sort of record for territorial government. During its long wait for admission, longer than Arizona's, New Mexico's well-wishers had plenty of time to suggest a host of secondary descriptive names by which this forty-seventh commonwealth might well be called.

Invariably, these hopeful suggestions were, like those for Arizona, flattering, among them being the Land of the Delight Makers, the Land of Heart's Desire, the Sunshine State, the Land of Opportunity, and the Colorful State. Meanwhile, too, the professional conjurers of happy phrases were improving. Long before the *New Mexico Magazine,* official periodical of the State Department of Development, made its bow, "The Land of Enchantment" was running front and center in its brilliant colors.

One should know that New Mexico represents a blend of three cultures. These are native Indian, Spanish, and American. Each has dominated. The composite influence which it now, after fifty years of statehood, presents on casual inspection, seems a harmonious picture. It is deceptive. The veneer of Americanization in many places runs thin indeed.

It is difficult to think of modern United States in a village of

Pueblo Indians praying and dancing for rain. And what tourist could dream of the "American Way of Life" while a Penitente flute is heard above the thud of the scourges while Spanish-Americans perform medieval rites of redemption during Holy Week?

These are extremes, but they are still to be seen in New Mexico, usually in the open country, diminishing near the larger towns, and vanishing altogether in some places. Little wonder if the state is a favorite camping ground of anthropologists. Here they can observe the living Indians in relation to their long unbroken past and possible future.

Even today, it is well that strangers learn the need to differentiate among the three racial elements. Before the United States occupation, the non-Indians of the region were, as persons of Spanish descent and subjects of Mexico, known as Mexicans. When the great influx of non-Spanish people occurred after 1848, the New Mexicans referred to them generally as "gringos." This carried no opprobrium. It meant simply any foreigner (save Spanish or Indian) who spoke Spanish without a good accent.

In time "gringo" came to carry a sneer chiefly—says Webster—as applied to Americans or Englishmen. It derives from a corruption of *griego,* Greek, familiar in Spain long before Mexicans came to use it.

At the time of annexation of the territory to the United States, the people of Spanish descent became United States citizens and were known thereafter as Spanish-speaking Americans to distinguish them from the Indians and the later emigrants from old Mexico. To distinguish the settlers from other parts of the United States, the prefix "Anglo" was added. Thus today's residents of the state are known as Spanish-Americans, Anglo-Americans, and Indians.

One should bear in mind, too, that in the migration annals of the United States, the general direction of movement was from east to west. In New Mexico, meaning in this instance, all the southwestern states originally embraced in the old Spanish province, that direction did not hold. For three centuries preceding the United States occupation, the trend of settlement here was all from the south. Contact with the outside world was not from the east or from the Atlantic seaboard, but from Mexico City and through Mexico from Spain.

After the close of our war with Mexico in 1848, and after a great deal of wrangling, a constitutional convention met in Santa Fe in 1850, and framed a constitution for the "state of New Mexico." But it was not to be so simple. Instead of a full-fledged member of the Union, the Territory of New Mexico emerged from the Congress and so it remained for more than six decades longer, through good times and bad times, or until 1912. By that time, the trend of settlement had long since been altered, and the main stream of migration had shifted. People were coming into New Mexico from the East, the West, and the North.

Early in the migration to New Mexico prompted by statehood was a lad of thirteen, who was to become one of the finest interpreters of all of the Southwest. Paul Horgan came from Buffalo, New York, in 1915, to live with his family in Albuquerque. He recalls that the city then had a population of somewhere around 12,000, and that the principal industries were the roundhouse and shops of the Santa Fe Railway and what he calls "the network of sanitoriums for tuberculosis patients." As in Colorado, therapy was a specialty.

In the still booming 1960s, New Mexico is no longer noted chiefly for its sunshine health resorts. It is minerals that now top its industrial index with a production of $648 million. Heading the values in fifty states, are uranium, potash, and perlite; and the state also stands high among those producing natural gas, pumice, manganese, copper, gold, and silver.

Second in New Mexico's economy is the United States Government with a payroll and expenditures topping $269 million. Tourism has taken third place with $216 million, beating agriculture, which accounts for more than $200 million. In respect to the latter item, Mr. Horgan recently remarked,[1] that on New Mexico ranches are herded more than a million head of cattle and a million head of sheep, and that visitors can see cowboys doing ranch chores on many major highways heading to the uranium mills.

This is significant. Mr. Horgan says that Americans now go West in order to go western, and that the real West has been replaced by "the infantile version of it." Meaning that the entire American public has accepted the West of big ranches, of cowboys, bad men, and all of the standard clichés of pulp paper, movies, and the films of TV shows.

There is no hiding place from the Westerns.

As author of *New Mexico's Own Chronicle,* and of other books about the Southwest, including *The Rio Grande,* Paul Horgan still makes his home in Roswell, where two outstanding events in local history occurred: In 1869, a professional gambler, Van C. Smith, arrived there, with his partner, Aaron O. Wilburn, to construct two adobe buildings, which served as post office and general store. Many years later, the first atomic bomb was exploded there, not far from Alamogordo; and the White Sands Proving Ground now forms part of the missile-testing range.

New Mexico is an old country and a new country. It has had a long infancy, leaving a great dizzying gap between the old and the new—from dim prehistory down to the memory of still living men. Creatures who were later to be named Llano man and Folsom man roamed the region. Through the ages it was subject to great and devastating droughts. In the thirteenth century one of the worst destroyed even the game; and the nomadic tribes that followed the game disappeared for a time. Primitive agriculture was wiped out.

"At some time or another," writes William Webber Johnson, in *The Romance of North America,* "the comparatively civilized aborigines of southern Mexico, who had developed their own arts and sciences to a high degree, moved north and east across

[1] *The Saturday Evening Post,* Jan. 23, 1962.

the land; and again the barbarous nomadic tribes moved southward into Mexico, only to collapse in fierce confusion before the wild Spaniard, Cortes, and his minuscule army."

Then, the Spanish explorers, whipped to frenzy by the gold and silver Cortes had seized from the Aztec ruler, Montezuma, made their first efforts into the seemingly empty country, hoping for another treasure. There followed mounted expeditions to find the storied wealth of Cibola and Gran Quivira. They prowled the deserts, the mountains and plains of the Southwest. They found the Grand Canyon of the Colorado; and traced the source of the Rio Grande. They marveled at the pueblos of the natives. And, one and all, they found nothing but grief. The cities of gold were to be found nowhere.

It was not until the first third of the nineteenth century that the westward bulge of the young United States began to be felt. The expansive, romantic nature of the fledgling nation, the old drives of desire for more land, or quick wealth, exerted a pressure that was to alter the entire region and, in the end, fill out the boundaries as we know them today.

To the west Santa Fe, one of the oldest settlements on the continent, became a busy trading center, a "crossroads for ambitious and adventurous impresarios." Freighters carried goods made of cloth and leather from eastern factories to places along the Santa Fe Trail. Other traders and, in increasing numbers, settlers, thronged the Osage Trace, the Texas road, and El Camino Real to San Antonio and the Rio Grande, or came by ship to Galveston Island, the headquarters of thieves and pirates, to work their way into the new country.

Land speculators were everywhere. So were their victims, the innocents, who had bought fake claims to lands in Texas from eastern con men, only to learn that they were "not deliverable in Texas but in Wall Street."

The War with Mexico, and the subsequent treaty that stemmed from it, were responsible for adding more than a quarter to what was later known as the continental United States, including much of what we now know as the Southwest. It comprised a vast area and, at one stroke, changed the maps that were to muddle geography for generations—California, Arizona, New Mexico, Nevada, and Utah. In return, the United States paid Mexico $15 million, or at the rate of less than three cents an acre. In the same month of 1848, in which Mexico ratified the treaty, gold, so long and unsuccessfully sought by Spaniards and Mexicans, was discovered in California. It was an irony, observed a Mexican with Latin fatalism, "We compromised. They took everything."

One thing is certain: New Mexico is not homogeneous. The Spanish settlement, with its roots in Chihuahua, spread like a tree up the central Rio Grande Valley, branching east and west; and today it is still the most prevalent influence in that part of the state. It is the only integral remnant of the northernmost fringe of Spanish empire in America.

Northeastern New Mexico, first penetrated from the east by trappers and traders and later developed by way of the Santa Fe Trail is today preponderantly Anglo-American. Railroads and mining turned the Anglo-Americans down the Rio Grande Valley and into the southwestern part of the state, where the Silver City complex of mines became the shipping point of the region. East central and southeastern New Mexico was first developed as cattle country soon after the Civil War. It was peopled largely by ranchers from Texas and is still markedly Texan in character. In the far northwest, the fertile San Juan Valley attracted Mormon homesteaders who, migrating south from Utah, established themselves in the region bordering the great Rocky Mountain plateau country which was then and today is also inhabited by Navaho Indians.

In the predominantly Anglo-American sections of New Mexico, the social life is much like that in other western states. In the central and northern sections, however, life is deeply colored by Spanish and Indian influences, which center primarily around the home and the church. Here they have combined with what many observers have termed "the tyrannical land" to perpetuate a fatalistic outlook as well as the old and proved ways of living.

The Civil War was responsible for abandonment, in 1861, of army posts, and concentration of Union forces at strategic points. Much of New Mexico Territory was exposed to attacks by Indians, who plundered settlements, massacred inhabitants, and ran off the livestock. Early in the war, Kit Carson, already known as a dispatch rider for pathfinder Frémont, and all-around scout and guide, helped to organize the First New Mexican Volunteer Infantry, of which he became colonel. Late in 1864, he, with some 400 men and two pieces of artillery, attacked 4000 Kiowas and Comanches at Adobe Walls, and after a desperate battle was forced to withdraw. But the tribes had learned to live on reservations. It was Kit Carson's last battle.

Kit Carson continued his efforts at subduing the wild lands until 1867, when he retired to live at Fort Lyon. He made his will and asked to be buried in Taos. An army physician put him on a diet, and forbade his pipe. Kit grumbled, and at last asked for a buffalo steak, a bowl of coffee, and his pipe. The doc said such a meal would kill him. "Don't matter," said Kit. He ate two pounds of steak, drank a quart of coffee, and smoked his pipe. He allowed he felt considerably better, and then he turned over and died very quietly. He got a funeral with full military honors, and his body was taken to Taos.

A local rumpus that went into New Mexico history as the "Lincoln County War," and made more headlines in the territory than did the Civil War, was a bloody feud that involved rival cattlemen and a hoodlum from Brooklyn called Billy the Kid. Territorial officials made little effort to put a stop to the feuding, and in 1878, President Hayes appointed General Lew Wallace Territorial Governor for the specific purpose of ending the Lincoln County War. (Wyoming had a Johnson County Range War.)

Governor Wallace set up his office in "a vile old chamber" of the fort at Santa Fe; but before he took the field, the "war" ended after some notable gunplay at, in and around the Lincoln County Court House at Lincoln. Billy the Kid fled after the battle at Lincoln; but was later removed from circulation by

Sheriff Pat Garrett, who performed a public service by shooting the sadistic thug at old Fort Sumner, seat of De Baca County. He has long since become one of the most sympathetic TV characters to come out of New Mexico.

Without making a point of it, New Mexico has come farther and changed more than any other of the western states. In Santa Fe is the Governor's Palace, built in 1610. In Taos are pueblos still older, some of which rise seven stories above the ground. The site of Albuquerque was first seen by white men when a detachment of Coronado's troops explored it in 1540.

Of change, what could be more basic than language? Until the 1930s all public business of the biennial legislature was conducted in both English and Spanish. English is now the official language of New Mexico.

If there were only some equation by which a state would be shown to have a vast area of land, compared to which was a minuscule population and, further, that a majority of the people were either painters or writers, then I am sure New Mexico would come off handsomely. The equation would read that the state has an area of 121,666 square miles, making it the fifth in size in the continental United States; and that its population was 951,023, or thirty-seventh in rank; and that from there on, the number of people who paint or write or do both is whatever the combined Chambers of Commerce of Taos, Santa Fe, and Albuquerque guess it to be.

This of course would be a fantastic number. It would represent not only the Indian spinners and weavers, who began to make blankets for export in the early eighteenth century, but also the Anglo-Americans who started dropping off in Taos almost a century later to begin what turned out to become the first New Mexican art colony. Meanwhile, production of the Taos Indian weavers rose and fell, then rose again, according to the popularity of native Indian blankets, and of artifacts like jewelry and pottery. For many years, both Indians and non-Indians have continued to produce arts and crafts until New

Mexico has become noted for its commerce in "artistic objects."

Non-Indian painters have led the parade. In 1914, those groups around Taos organized the Taos Society of Artists, which held regular spring and autumn exhibits in the art centers of New York, Boston, and Philadelphia. Some ten years later, a group called the New Mexican Painters was formed to include both the Taos and the Santa Fe colonies. A collector named Burt Harwood erected an art gallery in Taos to house the pictures and art objects he had bought, which he left to the town as an art center and which, on his death was named the Harwood Foundation and was taken over by the University of New Mexico, then renamed the Taos School of Art.

Then the gates really began to open—Los Canco Pintores; Art Leagues; the Transcendental Group; the Non-Objectives. It must have seemed that New Mexico had attracted painters from every last "school" anybody had heard of. Gallup, Melrose, Roswell soon had art centers, and other small communities became art conscious, what with art workshops, lectures, and classes in painting and sculpture.

This is not to say that the development of New Mexican art amounted to a Renaissance. Much of it was, naturally, derivative. But that it happened at all in New Mexico is almost incredible to visitors from longer settled places such as, say, Oregon, California, or Colorado.

By the time New Mexico went into its first boom in painting, it had long since produced a body of literature that was known to and widely read by Americans. But writing, good or bad, is generally accepted as something Americans can and will do. There is no astonishment about it. It is different with painting. This is a talent suspiciously like magic, and is generally believed to be given to few. Little wonder if tourists of even moderate sophistication are astonished with what they see in the many galleries and art centers scattered everywhere in New Mexico.

The first poet to become identified with New Mexico was Albert Pike, who also wrote the words to "Dixie," and in 1831 visited the region and romanticized *The Bold Navaho*. And in

1844 Josiah Gregg published his *The Commerce of the Prairies,* still a classic of the Santa Fe Trail. H. H. Bancroft did not overlook *Arizona and New Mexico,* which appeared in 1889. Emerson Hough wrote novels introducing the cowboy, the prospector, and other characters who became standard fare in books on the Southwest; and early in the new century Eugene Manlove Rhodes, a genuine working cowboy, began to write books that will outlive the rank and file of mere Westerns.

Harvey Fergusson, grandson of Santa Fe Trail pioneers, produced *Blood of the Conquerors,* perhaps the first realistic novel of contemporary New Mexico, and Willa Cather's *Death Comes for the Archbishop* told of the French priests whose advent in the 1850s did much to change the scene in Taos and elsewhere in New Mexico. Oliver LaFarge's *Laughing Boy: A Navaho Romance* won the Pulitzer Prize in 1929. In 1954 Paul Horgan's two volumes on the Rio Grande appeared, to be awarded both the Pulitzer and the Bancroft prizes in American history. An Englishman, D. H. Lawrence, thought by some to be a genius, lived for a time in Taos, and had at least three books written about him.

Though New Mexicans are proud of their contributions to culture in the fields of art, literature, and music, they do not forget that they live in a region designated as part of the Great American Desert. They know that the social and industrial use of water has increased so greatly that the outlook has raised no little concern.

But then, New Mexicans are said to be temperamentally optimistic—as why shouldn't a people be who live so near Alamogordo, and the White Sands National Monument? Could not atomic power be used to convert sea water into fresh water, and deliver it by pipeline to the desert regions? The possibility has been endlessly discussed.

One thing is certain: New Mexicans and visitors alike seem to enjoy the desert regions as they are. For instance, since 1930, when the Carlsbad Caverns were established as a national park, visitors have passed the half-million mark. Others come especially to see the remains of ancient peoples, of the Aztec Ruins National Monument, and the largest single ruin in the park system, which is that of Pueblo Bonito, in Chaco Canyon.

These things, however, are no more than a generous sample of the wonders storied in New Mexico's vast and gorgeous outdoor museum. There are the Gila Cliff Dwellings, the Bandelier National Monument, near Santa Fe; the El Morro National Monument, out of Albuquerque, and Capulin Mountain, not far from Raton in the northeastern part of the state; and, finally, the all but incredible White Sands National Monument, Alamogordo. They really do not need watering.

COLORADO

Chapter Eleven

Because it was admitted to the Union on August 1, 1876, one hundred years after the Declaration of Independence, Colorado is officially the Centennial State. It is also incomparably the Highest State. With peaks rising 10,000 feet or more, it has a mean altitude of 6600 feet, exceeding that of any other. Of the eighty peaks in North America that soar above 14,000 feet, Colorado has fifty-four.

Down the very middle of the state winds the Continental Divide, splitting it into two roughly equal sections, the Eastern and the Western Slope. More than a million and a half visitors come to see this ridgepole of the Rockies every year, and refresh themselves amid the high mountain scenery. The Rocky Mountain National Park is the most heavily visited of all our parks along the Divide, outranking Glacier, Grand Teton, and even Yellowstone in popularity. This park is said to be "the perfect family-type relaxing ground," offering a combination of nature in the raw, plus the latest thing in "outdoor conveniences."

Back in 1806, young Lieutenant Zebulon Montgomery Pike, here on an Army expedition to determine the southwestern boundary of the Louisiana Purchase, paused near the present site of Pueblo to observe with interest the great mountain peak which he had seen hanging like a white cloud on the horizon to the north. Then, lightly clothed and with little food, Pike and his men fought their way upward in a blizzard, but failed to reach the summit. This was the peak that has borne his name ever since, and became the most noted landmark in Colorado, after the "Pikes Peak or Bust" excitement of the 1858 gold rush to the diggings of Cherry Creek, which became Denver.

Yet, Pikes is not the highest elevation. That belongs to Long's Peak, at 14,255 feet, which Francis Parkman saw in 1846 but did not climb because, as he noted in *The Oregon Trail,* he did not think it was worth risking his scalp, and the region was then in the game-rich hunting grounds of the local tribes.

Today, the region is readily available. It is preserved in a more or less wild state in the Rocky Mountain National Park, a favorite starting point for tourists. You reach it by heading up US Route 34 through Big Thompson Canyon west of Loveland, Colorado, to Estes Park, a thriving commercial resort community just outside the park's main gates. This was the way that reporter Paul Schubert recently approached it on a tour of Colorado's high places (for *The Saturday Evening Post* in the summer of 1961).

Though there were no longer any scalp-hunting Indians along the way, reporter Schubert discovered several ambushes for unwary tourists. These included trading posts, beer joints, kiddie rides, and brilliantly illuminated motels. These were all outside the park gates, where you paid one dollar for a fifteen-day car permit for the park, and "drove into a landscape that is protected from most but not all of the effects of our mechanized, electrified civilization."

The highway is one of the park's concessions to modern tourists. Handy to this sky-touching road are big, permanent campgrounds with running water and flush toilets. The rocky slopes are crisscrossed with well-marked trails for hikers and horseback riders. Joel Estes, for whom Estes Park was named, was the first settler when, in 1860, he built a cabin on Fish Creek.

By 1865, campers had started to pitch their tents in the region, and five years later there was a stage line. Estes moved his family out of the park because, he said, "too many people were cluttering up the outdoors."

Worse was to come. In about 1871, the Earl of Dunraven, yachtsman, hunter, explorer, author, and war correspondent for the London *Daily Telegraph*, purchased 6000 acres in Estes Park and constructed a lodge, where he entertained English nobility and Americans.

But much of the popularity of the country must be credited to plain Enoch Mills, who spent his life climbing peaks, and writing books describing the grandeur of Colorado. His was probably the first to campaign to have it set aside as a national park, which was done in 1915, by congressional act. It now comprises 259,556 acres.

In this immense area a profusion of wild flowers carpets the high mountain meadows. They number more than 700 varieties, and early and late, something is always in bloom. The columbine, the state flower, blooms all summer, on the lower levels in June, and on the higher in September. Mariposa lilies, phlox, Indian paint-brush, asters, and marigolds are found in abundance. In the high marshy regions are patches here and there of bog orchids.

Deer, elk, and the Rocky Mountain or bighorn sheep are numerous. During hot weather they retreat to the heights and are seldom seen. Colder weather drives them to lower levels, where they graze along the edges of the highway. The park still has a few bears and cougars, and there are many types of smaller animals. Aspen groves near streams attract beavers.

Within the park 283 species of birds have been identified. These include the bluebird, wren, hermit thrush, hummingbird, and white-crowned sparrow; the ouzel, Rocky Mountain jay, chickadee, woodpecker, and magpie. Higher up are the rosy finch and the ptarmigan, the latter's color changing to snow-white in winter. Bird watchers are everywhere. At one of Trail Ridge Road's parking places, reporter-tourist Schubert saw a teen-age girl offer bread to a Clark's nutcracker, and her dad, who was an ornithologist at Harvard, told Schubert that the family had just arrived at the park on their first visit West. Later that afternoon, he saw a whole column of cars stop to disgorge a studious-looking group which proved to be the Plant Science Seminar of the American Society of Pharmacognosy. This science, he learned, deals with drugs, including those derived from plants. In another moment, clusters of highbrow males and females were down on hands and knees peering at tundra vegetation through magnifying glasses, while "others grouped around a green-uniformed Park naturalist who lectured learnedly on botany at 12,000 feet."

Like so many other western states, Colorado got its start, so to speak, by reason of a gold rush in 1858, when prospectors began modest placer operations in the Cherry Creek diggings that became Denver. A year later, a "loner" named George Jackson struck it rich in the mountains some thirty miles to the west, and then on May 9, 1859, John Gregory hit a real jackpot on the North Fork of Clear Creek, and the new camps of Blackhawk and Central City led the state in gold production for more than thirty years, or until the 1890s, when Cripple Creek surpassed everything that had gone before.

By 1874, the richest placer deposits were petering out, but one of the former gold camps, Leadville, was discovered to be rich in lead and silver. It went into a boom that suddenly brought 30,000 people to Leadville and also brought profound change in the industry. Instead of wild speculation, the Leadville camps turned hard-rock mining into a business. Before 1878, the production of all metal mines in Colorado had never exceeded $8 million annually. Then, after Leadville got going, silver production reached a peak of $23 million in 1892.

Although mining is generally presumed to be Colorado's basic industry, agriculture has produced almost twice as much of the state's yearly income. The mines have yielded more than

$3 billion since the gold rush of 1858, but agriculture has done almost as well within the past thirty-five years. In the larger sense, however, the two are complementary; neither could have achieved the present development without the other.

It is probable, with the advent of tourism, estimated as now bringing more than $360 million (AAA estimate 1960) into the state's coffers annually, that no small part of this sizable total is due to the attractions of Colorado's incomparable Ghost Towns on the Mine-Camp Circuit.

Call the roll almost anywhere in the high hills and in the deep canyons, and some voice will shout answer—answer *now*, in 1962—that this is Cripple Creek, or Creede, or Telluride, or Central City, or Black Hawk, or Leadville, or Aspen, or Ouray, Silverton . . . In one or in all of them there are surviving relics that will conjure up to even the least perceptive and unimaginative visitor what went on here in the days when gold, or silver, or lead, or perhaps copper was being lifted from the ground to make fortunes for a few, and wages for the many.

Volcanoes had piled up the hills. Steaming hot waters from deep in the earth percolated to the surface, bearing gold telluride in solution with quartz. The whole area presented a rough, gaunt aspect of barren rocky ridges, almost arid, with sudden valleys marked by scrub trees and, in season, a wealth of alpine flowers. These brief patches of brilliance, however, did little to soften the feeling that here one was in an appalling sort of country. Grim and bitter country. It was not, as one observer remarked, a place to invite human habitation.

Yet sixty years ago, Cripple Creek, for instance, meant three things—a stream, a city, and a mining district. The stream wasn't much, yet 25,000 people lived in Cripple Creek city along its banks. Another 20,000 lived in several smaller towns nearby. And in that year the district alone produced $17 million in gold, bringing the total for a decade to $111,361,633. It was then and for a few more years one of the biggest gold camps on earth.

Go look at it today, stranger, for it is well worth looking at; and so is almost any other of a dozen old mine districts that were the Colorado of yesterday.

But the visitor to Colorado should know that contrary to popular belief, the state is not wholly mountainous. Somewhere there has to be room for that agriculture which, in recent years has produced "almost twice as much income as has mining." Northeast across the Colorado plains angles the South Platte River; southwest, the Arkansas. Between their fertile and cultivated valleys, run bright green ribbons threading a brown expanse. Here lies a vast dry farming area, crisscrossed by uncounted thousands of miles of barbed wire, checkered with farms, and dotted here and there with the green oasis of a prairie hamlet shading itself from a truly blistering sun under trees that have been as carefully transplanted and tended as garden flowers.

Here the rainfall is scant, seldom attaining the annual state average of fifteen inches. Winds are high. Now and then a tornado whirls terrifyingly across these flat lands that were homesteaded two or three generations ago, to leave them in a condition close to the dust bowls of the true Plains states. In spite of which, wrote an observer, "these weather-beaten plainsmen, bred to the earth, continue to grow crops and graze stock in spite of drought, wind, insect plagues, and occasional devastating hailstorms."

The first irrigation on a large scale began in 1870 with the founding of the Union Colony at Greeley. Sponsored by and named for Horace Greeley, editor of the New York *Tribune,* this co-operative effort dug the first big canal in the state. It was highly successful. Big ditches soon became a regular thing. The land was partitioned into water districts; reservoirs were dug to catch and hold the spring flow of rivers and creeks; and before long the federal government lent a hand.

The largest single enterprise based on irrigation came into being late last century, with the cultivation of sugar beets from

Germany. After experimental plantings near Grand Junction, sugar beets spread until only potatoes matched them as the staple crop of Colorado farms. Today, the industry operates many refineries throughout the state, and field workers commonly of Mexican background are employed by the many thousands. They migrate according to need, and their camps in season are perhaps the most picturesque scenes to be found in the state.

In addition to sugar beets, the irrigated sections grow wheat, and rye; and on both irrigated and dry farms, corn, oats, and grain sorghums are raised primarily as feed crops. Pinto beans have become an important cash crop on the plains. Much hay, the state's chief crop, is cut from natural meadows in the mountains; alfalfa, clover, timothy, sweet sorghum, and wild hay are the principal varieties.

As elsewhere, the steady improvements of refrigeration in railroad cars and motor trucks have greatly widened the markets for apples, peaches, and pears. Jefferson County and other areas near Denver are the berry patch of Colorado, and supply the local markets. Berries are also grown along the Grand Mesa in Garfield County; and Glenwood Springs on the upper Colorado River is noted for its mountain strawberries. Then there is the Rocky Ford cantaloupe, famous throughout the country; and honeydew melons and winter watermelons are a big crop in the Arkansas River Valley.

Celery has long since become the state's most widely noted vegetable. Much of it is wrapped with paper to bleach in the field and then stored in trenches for further bleaching for the holiday market.

At the corner of East Platte and North Nevada avenues, in Colorado Springs, there is an equestrian statue of General William Jackson Palmer. No man contributed more to Colorado than this veteran of the Civil War and holder of the Congressional Medal of Honor. He came to the state in charge of construction of the Union Pacific, but soon left it to join the new Denver & Rio Grande as first president. A long struggle with the Santa Fe resulted in his reorganization of the new line as the Denver & Rio Grande Western. It was to have a narrow-gauge track, 3 feet wide instead of the conventional 4 feet, 8½ inches. This would cost less for construction, and permit it to make sharp curves and to climb steeply. (Remember, Palmer knew he must cross the Rockies.)

He got under way with his Denver & Rio Grande Western late in 1870, and the line was completed in 1901, when he sold his interest to the parent company. Meanwhile, however, Palmer had been a prime mover in the founding and development of Colorado Springs. He helped to found Colorado College. He organized the Colorado Coal and Iron Company, and laid out the town of Bessemer, now part of Pueblo. Any one of these efforts would have marked Palmer as an unusual man; and Colorado Springs alone indicated his ability to attract and influence "the most outrageous and colorful collection of people ever seen in the Rocky Mountains."[1] Among them were the numerous and brilliant Penrose family of Philadelphia, including Charles Bingham, Richard Alexander Fullerton, Dr. Richard, Senator Boies, and Spencer, along with in-laws and close friends who took to Colorado Springs and stuck there as though they were integral if movable parts of the gorgeous scenery.

Added to these Philadelphians were the English colony to make the Springs into a "Little London"; and the Bostonians who gave direction to Colorado College. Taken as a permanent unit, these well-heeled people, and more like them, turned Colorado Springs into the largest of American spas. It was nothing like Newport or Saratoga, nothing like Bar Harbor or Palm Beach. It is impossible to characterize it. Let us say only that its founders planned a community to attract and hold people of means and social standing, a citizenry of "good moral character and strict temperance habits." It was made clear that manufac-

[1] For an excellent and detailed account of Colorado Springs, and what it has meant and still means to Colorado, see Marshall Sprague's *Newport in the Rockies, the Life and Good Times of Colorado Springs,* Sage Books, Denver, 1961.

turing establishments were not desired. Mills, smelters, saloons, and gambling houses were to be confined to Colorado City. General William J. Palmer, promoter of the Denver & Rio Grande Railroad, was impressed with this townsite so near the mountains and the foothill canyons. His company bought 10,000 acres at a dollar an acre, and on July 31, 1871, the first stake was driven at what is now the southeast corner of Pikes Peak and Cascade avenues. Three months later the tracks of the Denver & Rio Grande Western Railroad, the first narrow-gauge line in the State, reached the prospective town from Denver.

Within a year a passable road had been built to the Springs from Manitou. A British journalist, Isabella A. Bird, traveled over it that fall: "After fording a creek," she wrote, "I came to a decayed looking cluster of houses bearing the arrogant name of Colorado City, and a few miles farther on I saw the bleak scattered houses of the ambitious watering-place of Colorado Springs . . . A queer embryo-looking place it is, out on the bare plains, yet rising and likely to rise, with some big hotels much resorted to."

Such was the beginning of what the railroad publicized as "a scenic wonderland" and health resort. (Pikes Peak was already a national landmark.) Physicians extolled the dry air and bright sunlight. Several tuberculosis sanatoriums were in the planning stage. The irrigation ditches bordering every street were in summer embossed with flowers. Ditch water was carried in tubs for domestic purposes, and clear cold drinking water was peddled about the streets at twenty-five cents a barrel. The fashionable afternoon promenade was to the post office.

As early as 1873, when the town had supplanted Colorado City as the county seat, it was finding favor with artists and writers, some of whom made their homes here. Among these was Helen Hunt Jackson, who was soon to write the famous *Ramona*.

During the late 1870s, the vanguard of young Englishmen came to settle and soon introduced golf, polo, and even cricket.

In 1882, the opening of the Antlers Hotel, the finest resort hotel in the mountain West, with all manner of gables and turrets and cozy balconies, was a sensation. It had a hydraulic elevator, public rooms had tons of Gothic furniture upholstered in leather. It had central heating and gaslights, and seventy-five guest rooms with two baths on each floor. General Palmer was highly pleased. His first hotel had charm and worldliness, and its fame spread, removing from the eastern mind any lingering doubts about the quality of this Newport in the Rockies, as Colorado Springs was soon to be known.

Forty years later, Willa Cather was writing a book (*A Lost Lady*) and wanted to stamp her central character with the special elegance of the place and period. So she wrote the "bewitching young Mrs. Forrester always wintered fashionably with her aging husband at the Antlers . . ."

The great energy expended by Palmer and half a dozen of his cronies set forces in motion that were to change Colorado Springs from what an observer termed "a quiet village for the exercise of genteel indolence" to a bustling though still genteel city, "hell-bent on progress with a Board of Trade and everything." Bank deposits increased. The population rose from 4500 in 1884 to 11,200 in 1890. Five railroads were now pounding through town. Electric streetcars had replaced horsecars. Several new resorts were building in the Ute Pass district. Salmon G. Simmons, the "bed maker" came to lay a cog railroad up Pikes Peak, a vertical climb of 7539 feet as compared to 4684 feet to the top of Mount Washington in New Hampshire, long since successful. John Hundley laid a carriage road up the same peak, and built a barn with a ventilating system for his one hundred horses. And then the spirit of enterprise was recognized when a local man put an immense billboard at the top of Pikes Peak to herald the arrival of Adam Forepaugh's Three-Ring Circus.

Colorado City was not standing still. It got the shops of the Colorado & Midland Railroad, already heading for the new silver camp at Aspen; it got Jerome Wheeler's Glass Works, which made gorgeous green pickle jars and whiskey flasks. And after the great gold strike at Cripple Creek, big reduction mills rose in Colorado City, and citizens pointed with pride to the more than thirty new saloons and gambling houses that were required to handle the booming population.

One of the great and most durable stories concerns that of Horace A. W. Tabor, a stonecutter from Vermont, who after twenty years of futile prospecting in the mine regions, was running a store and acting as postmaster at Oro City where he had grubstaked a couple of German shoemakers with seventeen dollars' worth of flour and bacon. The story is familiar. Within hours, the two men had struck the enormous Chrysolite lode, later developed as the Little Pittsburgh in the Leadville district. Tabor's one-third interest brought him dividends of $500,000. Within a year, he had sold out, and invested his profits in the even richer Matchless Mine.

Then, with a fortune estimated at $9 million, Tabor embarked on a career that has been the source of more books than can readily be believed. He got into politics; built opera houses and imposing business buildings in Leadville and Denver; and divorced his wife, whom he had married in Maine, and married Elizabeth McCourt ("Baby") Doe, young, beautiful, and a divorcee, who had attracted his eye in early Leadville days. Among those attending the wedding party at the Willard Hotel, Washington, was President Chester A. Arthur.

It didn't last. In 1893 came a sudden panic; silver prices collapsed, banks closed, and Tabor's empire crumbled. Before he died, in 1899, he cautioned Baby Doe to "Hang on to the Matchless." And this she did, living alone in a shack beside the mine in poverty until her death in 1935. By that time, even the storied mines of Leadville and Cripple Creek had long passed their peak.

Off and on for many years, there had been strife in the camps. Periodically the towns had been rocked by dynamite and gunplay in the continuing war between the Western Federation of Miners and the Mine Operators Association. One night in 1902, the railroad depot at Independence, near Cripple Creek, was blown to pieces, leaving thirteen dead and twenty-four badly injured. At a meeting in Victor, five miners were shot down. Others were killed by rifle and shotgun fire. A sort of climax came, not in Colorado, but Caldwell, Idaho, where the governor of the state was blown to bits in front of his home.

Arrested and charged with the murder was Harry Orchard, a professional dynamiter, who confessed to have killed twenty persons in Colorado, including the job at Independence. William Haywood, head of the Western Federation, was arrested in Colorado as an accomplice and taken to Idaho, where he was successfully defended by Clarence Darrow. Orchard went to prison, where he served to his death in 1954, when he was eighty-three years old.

But the violence in Colorado's mine districts continued. In 1914, during a strike of coal miners, shooting broke out in Ludlow, and several strikers were killed during a battle with units of the National Guard. The strike was lost, but the issue aroused public opinion. A monument to the "Ludlow Massacre" marks the spot.

Although the labor-capital wars are now things long past, the old camps continue to be unmatched as tourist magnets. And at least one railroad survives to amaze and delight visitors with the Silverton Train. This operates daily during summer months on the narrow-gauge Denver & Rio Grande out of Durango (altitude, 6505) to Silverton (altitude, 9302), in the center of the San Juan mining region.

The Silverton Train has become one of the most celebrated tourist attractions in all the Rocky Mountains. During the 1961 season, it was running filled to capacity and with waiting lines of applicants for space in its decrepit yellow wooden coaches.

In terms of revenue per passenger mile, it was the most profitable railroad operation in the United States.

In this day of almost universal automotive transportation, one can scarcely think of a more welcome survival than the Silverton Train of the Denver & Rio Grande . . .

BIBLIOGRAPHY

American Guide Series, 1937–1950.

Ballantine, Bill, "A New Shunpike Tour—The Mormon Country," *Holiday,* March 1961.

The Book of Mormon, An Account Written by the Hand of Mormon upon Plates Taken from the Plates of Nephi, Salt Lake City, Utah, Published by The Church of Jesus Christ of Latter-day Saints, 1950.

Burt, Struthers, *Powder River, Let 'er Buck,* New York, 1938.

Cahn, Robert, "The New Utah: Change Comes to Zion," *The Saturday Evening Post,* April 1, 1961.

Cleland, Robert Glass, *From Wilderness to Empire,* New York, 1944. *Dictionary of American Biography,* 23 vols., New York.

De Voto, Bernard, *The Year of Decision: 1846,* Boston, 1953.

Highsmith, Richard H., ed., *Atlas of the Pacific Northwest,* Oregon State University Press, Corvallis, Oregon, 1962.

Holbrook, Stewart H., *Far Corner,* New York, 1952.

Holbrook, Stewart H., *The Story of American Railroads,* New York, 1944.

Horgan, Paul, *New Mexico's Own Chronicle* (with Maurice Garland Fulton), 1937.

Howard, Joseph Kinsey, *Montana, High, Wide and Handsome,* New Haven, 1944.

Hungerford, Edward, *Wells Fargo,* New York, 1953.

Lewis, Oscar, *Sagebrush Casinos,* New York, 1955.

Lewis, Oscar, *Silver Kings,* New York, 1947.

McArthur, Lewis A., *Oregon Geographic Names,* Portland, 1944.

Marcosson, Isaac F., *Anaconda,* New York, 1957.

Meany, Edmond, *History of the State of Washington,* New York, 1910.

Morris, Joe Alex, "Arizona: Airconditioned Desert," *The Saturday Evening Post,* June 17, 1961.

Nadeau, Remi, "Baghdad on the Freeway," *American Heritage,* August, 1958.

National Geographic Society, America's Playgrounds, The National Parks, Washington, D.C., 1959.

Tilden, Freeman, *The National Parks,* New York, 1951.

The Romance of North America, ed. Hardwick Moseley, Boston, 1958.

Parrish, Philip H., *Before the Covered Wagon,* Portland, 1934.

Quiett, Glenn C., *Pay Dirt,* New York, 1936.

Smith, Harold S., *I Want to Quit Winners,* New York, 1961.

Sprague, Marshall, *Newport in the Rockies,* Denver, 1961.

Toole, K. Ross, *Montana, An Uncommon Land,* Norman, Oklahoma, 1959.

Willison, George F., *Here They Dug the Gold,* New York, 1946.

Wright, J. F. C., *Slava Bohu* (The Dukhobors), Toronto, 1940.

Wolle, Muriel Sibell, *The Bonanza Trail,* Bloomington, Indiana, 1953.

Wolle, Muriel Sibell, *Stampede to Timberline, The Ghost Towns and Mining Camps of Colorado,* Boulder, Colorado, 1949.

Oct 25 1964

Lupe A. [illegible]elley.